Tom Tiddler's Ground

Tom Tiddler's Ground, Leonard Clark tells us, is "that no-man's-land where gold and silver can be picked up just for the asking." And Walter de la Mare regarded the world of poetry as the richest kind of Tom Tiddler's Ground. He says in his Introduction:

"To learn to love books and reading is one of the very best things that can happen to anybody. So, too, with pictures and music. Poetry in particular *wears* well. The longer you care for it in itself the better it gets. You can see the spring's first tuft of primroses, or watch a tom-tit with a nut, or the evening star, or the kitchen fire, or a pond in the moonlight, or your mother's face, or even a cat washing her own—you can do all these things ninety-nine times and still find them as new and lively and odd and mysterious and interesting at the hundredth. And so it is with old rhymes and all the old tales and poems one cares for most. Love them once, you love them always."

Borzoi Books
for young people by
WALTER
DE LA MARE
Come Hither
Jack and the Beanstalk
A Penny a Day
Stories from the Bible
Tales Told Again
The Three Royal Monkeys
Peacock Pie
The Magic Jacket

TOM TIDDLER'S GROUND

A book of poetry
for children chosen
and annotated by

WALTER DE LA MARE

with a foreword by
Leonard Clark
and drawings by
Margery Gill

Alfred A. Knopf: New York

L. C. catalog card number: 62-9471

THIS IS A BORZOI BOOK,
PUBLISHED BY ALFRED A. KNOPF, INC.

Illustrations Copyright © 1961 by The Bodley Head.
Foreword Copyright © 1961 by Leonard Clark.

FIRST AMERICAN EDITION

2 164

The publishers have made every effort to trace the ownership of the copyright material in this book. It is their belief that the necessary permissions from publishers, authors and authorized agents have been obtained, but in the event of any question arising as to the use of any material, the publishers, while expressing regret for any error unconsciously made, will be pleased to make the necessary correction in future editions of this book.

Thanks are due to the following for permission to reprint copyright material:

The Society of Authors and Miss Pamela Hinkson for *Lambs* by Katharine Tynan; Messrs. Michael Joseph, Ltd., and the author for *For a Dewdrop, A Catching Song* and *Shadows* from *Silver-sand and Snow* by Eleanor Farjeon; The Oxford University Press and the author for *One Lime* and *Mary and her Kitten* from *The Children's Bells* by Eleanor Farjeon; The Oxford University Press for *The Inky Boys* and *The Story of Augustus* from *Struwelpeter* by Heinrich Hoffman; Miss D. E. Collins for *The Children's Song of the Nativity* by Frances Chesterton; Messrs. Secker and Warburg, Ltd., for *The Old Ships* by the late James Elroy Flecker; Mrs. H. M. Davies and Messrs. Jonathan Cape, Ltd., for *The Rain* by W. H. Davies; *Four-Paws* by Helen Parry Eden is reprinted by permission of *Punch;* Messrs. Wells Gardner, Darton & Co., Ltd., for *The Windmill* by the late E. V. Lucas; the estate of the late E. H. W. Meyerstein for *England;* Messrs. Dodd, Mead & Company, New York, and Messrs. McClelland and Stewart, Toronto, for *Winter Streams* from *Poems* by Bliss Carman; Captain Francis Newbolt, C.M.G., for *Against Oblivion* from *Poems Old and New* by Sir Henry Newbolt, published by Messrs John Murray (Publishers), Ltd., and *The Deserted House* by Mary Coleridge; The Macmillan Company for: *Weathers* and *Men Who March Away* from *Collected Poems* by Thomas Hardy, copyright 1925 by The Macmillan Company; and *Stupidity Street* and *Bells of Heaven* from *Poems* by Ralph Hodgson, copyright 1917 by The Macmillan Company, renewed 1945 by Ralph Hodgson; Mr. Raglan Squire, Messrs. Macmillan & Co., Ltd., and the Macmillan Company of Canada, Ltd., for *The Ship* from *Collected Poems* by the late Sir John Squire; Mrs. Shanks, Messrs. Macmillan & Co., Ltd., and the Macmillan Company of Canada, Ltd., for *The Storm* from *Poems 1912–1932* by Edward Shanks; Miss Beatrice Eve for *The Shower;* Miss Molly McArthur for *Secrets;* Miss Irene McLeod for *Lone Dog;* and the Executors of the late Herbert Jonathan Cape for *The First Bee* by Mary Webb.

Foreword

I listened, I opened,
I looked to left and right,
(*Some One*, Walter de la Mare)

When, in 1923, Walter de la Mare published *Come Hither*, 'a collection of rhymes and poems for the young of all ages', it was the first of all the distinguished anthologies he was to compile during his long and fruitful life. What made that particular collection of English romantic poetry so outstanding was that it was compiled by a great poet, a master himself of the romantic lyric, with a prodigious knowledge of the highways and byways of English poetry. Even now, forty years later, *Come Hither* continues to hold its own and to entrance newer generations with its haunting magic.

A very wide range of poems of high quality—many of them of immortal endurance—was assembled by Walter de la Mare between the covers of *Come Hither*, though he included no work by himself in the first edition. There were also over 170 pages of personal and very informative notes (about a quarter of the whole book) which gave the anthology added weight and authority. Nothing on so large and detailed a scale had ever before been attempted by an editor of Walter de la Mare's stature for 'the young of all ages'.

Come Hither was the poetic godparent of *Tom Tiddler's Ground*. It was Walter de la Mare's fame as a poet, and as an anthologist, which led the firm of Collins to invite him, in 1930, to prepare a book of poetry suitable for children.

Walter de la Mare was greatly attracted by the prospect and took a great deal of trouble with it. The result was an exciting little collection which, though deliberately narrower in aim and more circumscribed because of the limits determined by the audience for which it was intended, was clearly of the same order as *Come Hither*. In fact, *Tom Tiddler's Ground* can be described as a miniature *Come Hither*. This is not to decry it but rather to explain its genesis.

So *Tom Tiddler's Ground* appeared. It was first published in October 1931, as three little books of 96 pages each; there was

5

also a one-volume edition. The booklets cost 1s. 6d. each, the single volume, 5s. The anthology was such a success that a second edition was soon called for. This came in 1932—and with forty pictorial decorations 'reproduced from the woodcuts of Thomas Bewick, the pioneer of the art of woodcut illustration'. Bewick himself had, on occasions, supplied his minute and fascinating woodcuts for nineteenth-century books of poetry for the young, but this must have been the first time in this century that his work had been used for an anthology for children. Bewick's work was hardly known at all by the general public and, at that time, was even out of fashion in art circles. It was just like Walter de la Mare to revive it and to reproduce the woodcuts in such a context.

It was typical of de la Mare, too, to give his anthology such an unexpected title. For 'Tom Tiddler's Ground' is that no-man's-land where gold and silver can be picked up just for the asking. 'Tiddler', at one time spelled 'tidler', is said to be the shortened form of 'the idler' or 't'dler'. And 'Tom Tiddler's Ground' is the name of a very old children's game, played, especially in the north of England, as soon as the New Year has begun. The rules of the game were very simple. A line was drawn on the ground and a boy was chosen (by one or other of the counting-out games) to be the Tom Tiddler. He took his stand behind the line, sometimes mounted on a pile of stones, to guard his territory. The other players in the game would then proceed to dash in, to invade his ground, shouting as they did so:

> 'Here I am on Tom Tiddler's ground
> Picking up gold and silver.'

Tom would have to do his best to repel them, not, one imagines, a very easy task if there were many of them on the foray. The phrase passed into the language and Charles Dickens referred to it at least twice in his books. In 1848 he wrote in *Dombey and Son*:

> 'The spacious dining room with . . . the glittering table . . .
> might have been taken for a grown-up exposition of Tom
> Tiddler's Ground where children pick up gold and silver.'

But there is little *real* gold and silver for children to pick up for nothing. Tom Tiddler's Ground is imaginary ground for them.

6

Of course, de la Mare knew this. Perhaps, too, he remembered A. C. Benson's remark in 1907, in his book *From a College Window*:

> 'I would rather regard literature as a kind of Tom Tiddler's Ground where there is gold as well as silver to be picked up.'

Walter de la Mare would certainly have regarded the world of poetry as the richest kind of Tom Tiddler's Ground because all the treasures of poetry are free and there for the asking. They are compounded, too, of the finest gold and silver, since they are the treasures of man's mind and spirit. But it is one thing to display the bounty of poetry but quite another for full advantage to be taken of the gift. Walter de la Mare makes this quite clear in his Introduction. Having warned us that the rhymes in his book give 'only a glimpse of the great feast of English poetry', he then invites us to 'go out into the wonderful riches of mind and heart' which that poetry reveals. But he tells us that he does not:

> 'know of any true poem, however difficult it may seem at the first reading of it, that has not become much clearer as soon as I have begun to *try* to understand it.'

If we are to pick up the everlasting gold and silver from *his* Tom Tiddler's Ground he says that it would be best:

> 'to find someone to help you who not only cares for it but has also had to find his or her way, and may in turn have been helped in doing so.'

And again:

> 'it is always good, so far as it is possible, to *understand* what one reads. A deep and vivid understanding only adds to the joy it gives.'

How true all this is and how fitting that a great poet should say it. For him, poetry was an art which gave lasting pleasure, which yielded up more knowledge and delight, as one became more familiar with its labyrinthine ways. There are no idlers loafing about in his Tom Tiddler's Ground.

Walter de la Mare said he could only 'give a glimpse' of poetry; and that is true, too. All the same, he chose over 230 pieces from the treasure chest, ranging from nursery rhymes and games rhymes of ancient origin, to poems by just over a dozen of

7

his own contemporaries. The lesser as well as the greater names were represented, for de la Mare included those poems he thought were suitable for his purpose, which he liked for themselves, and not because of the distinction, or otherwise, of their writers. Yet *Tom Tiddler's Ground* gives us a very solid and revealing cross-section of English poetry, as authentic and appealing today as ever.

And how like de la Mare himself are the notes which he wrote for 138 of the poems. Sometimes he added a few words to the easier rhymes and sometimes two whole pages, which is what he does for Shelley's *The Question*. We should observe, too, how cunningly the anthology is put together. There are groupings of similar poems, one poem suggests another, there are more detailed notes for the more difficult poems, the longer poems have been placed towards the end of the book. It is a unique experience merely to read the book right through as it stands, without any picking and choosing of favourite poems. 'The young of all ages' will be well-informed, indeed, who *know* the inspired contents of this anthology. For it is not only a fine collection of English poetry; it is also a Walter de la Mare collection. Perhaps the two are synonymous. Its good sense, as far as poetry is concerned, and its sure understanding of what the young enjoy, cannot be dated. And now, thirty years after the original date of publication, it appears in this new edition with its careful production and charming decorations by Margery Gill. For those who want poems which are written in our own day there are other anthologies. But there is only one *Tom Tiddler's Ground*. As there was only one Walter de la Mare

'Sighing a beauty
Secret as dream.'

Leonard Clark

8

CONTENTS

13

15

Introduction

There are many kinds of rhymes in this book—mere jingles, game-rhymes, nursery rhymes and poems. Some are old, some are new. Some are rather roughly made, they jog and stumble when they ought to dance; others are among the most lovely and perfect things that have ever been made out of English words. But every one has its own kind of goodness, and gives its own kind of pleasure, and many of them I have loved since I was a child.

None the less, this is only a little book. It gives only a glimpse of the great feast of English poetry. But that is much. There was once an Irishman who made a henhouse for his chickens. When it was finished, he cut a large hole in the door for his full-sized hens to go in at and to come out of—and a little hole for the chicks! Still, whichever one they used, they *all came out*.

They all came out into the same great farmyard—with its ricks and its barns and its moss-grown stones, and its grass and its pigs and its geese and its ducks and its wild birds, and its fields and meadows over the wall. And the woods beyond *them*, and the hills beyond them, and the blue sky with its clouds and skylarks beyond and above them too. And so into the full light of the morning. In the same way, from the rhymes and poems in this book, you can go out into the wonderful riches of mind and heart revealed in our great English poetry.

Not all the poems in it are merry, lively and sparkling, not all are so plain and simple that they almost sing themselves. There are enough of these, however, to prove that poetry is not dry or dull or something you have to wait to enjoy until you are grown up. Why, even babies of three can chirrup and dance to 'Mary, Mary!' and to 'Old King Cole.' Some of the poems are serious, some are tragic; many are easy to understand, a few will be difficult. But I do not know of any true poem, however sorrow-ful it may be, that is not a comfort to read and to remember and a good deal else beside. Nor do I know of any true poem, however difficult it may seem at the first reading of it, that has not become much clearer as soon as I have begun to *try* to understand it. Some poems may always remain difficult; and there are many other things in life and in books that only the wisest can understand. Still, one can at least try to understand, and as a wise friend who loves both poetry and children once said to me, it is often what seem to be the simplest things that most need explaining.

We can, too, and particularly when we are young, delight in the sound of the words of a poem, immensely enjoy them—the music and rhythm and lilt, feel its enchantment and treasure it in memory, without realising its *full* meaning—just as we can listen to a wren or blackbird singing without knowing what that singing means.

It is best, therefore, to try to find your way in a poem for yourself. It is next best to find someone to help you who not only cares for it but has also had to find his or her way, and may in turn have been helped in doing so. In this book I have tried, where it seemed wanted, and very often when I wanted it myself, to give this help.[1]

Apart from meaning, many questions may be asked about poems, the answers to which will be full of interest and yet not necessary to the enjoyment of the poems. Why, for example, Old King Cole called for three fiddlers and not for seven; who— *if* he was ever anybody else—Jack Horner[2] really was; why such and such a line of a poem is good grammar though it may not seem so; when any particular poem was written, and what kind of man the writer was; and last, why one *ought* to like it. All such knowledge may be interesting and valuable, but it is not necessary to one's delight; and there are very few 'oughts' in regard to the love of poetry. Let your eyes, mind, heart and spirit feed on it, and see what happens.

Nevertheless, it is always good, so far as it is possible, to *understand* what one reads. A deep and vivid understanding only adds to the joy it gives, and a few words may clear away a difficulty.

[1] Here and there a word or two has been altered in some old rhyme of which there are many variants, and I have occasionally put in a stop in the hope of making the sound or the sense of a line a little clearer. When accents appear it is only to show how it seemed to me the line should run; but there may be more than one good way of reading any particular line.

[2] Georgie Porgie, for example, who kissed the girls and made them cry, once wore a crown; and there was one waiting for Charley 'over the water', though he never put it on his head.

Where, however, in the pages that follow, there seems to be no difficulty and there is yet an explanation, the explanation can easily be left unread. Besides, I may not always have given the right explanation! In any case always go back to the poem again after reading anything that may have been said about it.

To learn to love books and reading is one of the very best things that can happen to anybody. So, too, with pictures and with music. Poetry in particular *wears* well. The longer you care for it in itself the better it gets. You can see the spring's first tuft of primroses, or watch a tom-tit with a nut, or the evening star, or the kitchen fire, or a pond in the moonlight, or a butterfly on a wild rose, or your mother's face, or even a cat washing her own —you can do all these things ninety-nine times and still find them as new and lively and odd and mysterious and interesting at the hundredth. And so it is with old rhymes and all the old tales and poems one cares for most. Love them once, you love them always.

Read slowly; *say* the words over either aloud or to yourself as you read; listen carefully to the sound of them as well as to the sense; try to see and hear in your mind all that the poem tells of; think while you read; and don't give any poem up merely because you fail to like it immediately. You never can tell; sooner or later there may come a moment when you will hear 'in the silence of morning the song of the bird'.

Walter de la Mare

The Winds they did Blow

The winds they did blow;
    The leaves they did wag;
Along came a beggar boy,
    And put me in his bag.

He took me up to London;
    A lady me did buy,
She put me in a silver cage,
    And hung me up on high,

With apples by the fire,
    And nuts for to crack,
Besides a little feather bed
    To rest my little back.

I had a Little Nut-Tree

I had a little nut-tree, nothing would it bear
But a silver nutmeg and a golden pear;
The King of Spain's daughter came to visit me,
And all was because of my little nut-tree.
I skipped over water, I danced over sea,
And all the birds in the air couldn't catch me.

Seeds

I sowed the seeds of love,
It was all in the Spring,
In April, May and sunny June,
When small birds they do sing.

Hee, Haw, Hum

Jòhn Còok had a little grey mare; *hee, haw, hum:*
Her back stood up, and her bones were bare; *hee, haw, hum.*

John Cook was rìding up Shùter's bank; *hee, haw, hum:*
And there his nag did kick and prank; *hee, haw, hum.*

John Cook was riding up Shuter's hill; *hee, haw, hum:*
His mare fell down, and she made her will; *hee, haw, hum.*

The bridle and saddle were laid on the shelf; *hee, haw, hum:*
If you want any more you may sing it yourself; *hee, haw,*
hum.

I had a Little Pony

I had a little pony,
  His name was Dapple-gray,
I lent him to a lady,
  To ride a mile away;
She whipped him, she slashed him,
  She rode him through the mire;
I would not lend my pony now
  For all the lady's hire.

There was a Monkey

There was a monkey climbed up a tree,
When he fell down, then down fell he.

There was a crow sat on a stone,
When he was gone, then there was none.

There was an old wife did eat an apple,
When she'd eat two, she'd eat a couple.

There was a horse a-going to the mill,
When he went on, he stood not still.

There was a butcher cut his thumb,
When it did bleed, the blood did come.

There was a lackey ran a race,
When he ran fast, he ran apace.

There was a cobbler clouting shoon,
When they were mended, they were done.

There was a chandler making candle,
When he them strip, he did them handle.

There was a navy went into Spain,
When it returned, it came again.

The Inky Boys

Heinrich Hoffman

As he had often done before,
The Woolly-headed Blackamoor
One nice fine summer's day went out
To see the shops and walk about;
And as he found it hot, poor fellow,
He took with him his green umbrella.

Then Edward, noisy little wag,
Ran out and laughed, and waved his flag;
And William came in jacket trim
And brought his wooden hoop with him;
And Arthur, too, snatched up his toys
And joined the other naughty boys;
So one and all set up a roar
And laughed and hooted more and more,
And kept on singing—only think!—
'Oh! Blacky, you're as black as ink!'

Now tall Agrippa lived close by—
So tall he almost reached the sky;
He had a mighty inkstand too,
In which a great goose-feather grew;
He called out in an angry tone:
'Boys! leave the Blackamoor alone!
For if he tries with all his might,
He cannot change from black to white.'
But, ah! they didn't mind a bit
What great Agrippa said of it;
And went on laughing as before,
And hooting at the Blackamoor.

Then great Agrippa foams with rage,
(Oh! could I draw him on this page!)
He seizes Arthur, seizes Ned,
Takes William by his little head;
And though they scream and kick and call,
Into the ink he dips them all;
Into the inkstand—one—two—three,
Till they are black as black can be;
And then they skip, and then they run!
The Blackamoor enjoys the fun.
They have been made as black as crows,
Quite black all over—eyes and nose,
And legs and arms and heads and toes,
And trousers, pinafores and toys—
The silly little inky boys!
Because they set up such a roar,
And teased the harmless Blackamoor.

Don't-Care

Don't-Care—he didn't care,
   Don't-Care was wild:
Don't-Care stole plum and pear
   Like any beggar's child.

Don't-Care was made to care,
   Don't-Care was hung:
Don't-Care was put in a pot
   And stewed till he was done.

The Pigs

Jane Taylor

'Do look at those pigs as they lie in the straw,'
   Willy said to his father one day;
'They keep eating longer than ever I saw,
   Oh, whàt greedy gluttons are they!'

'I see they are feasting,' his father replied,
   'They eat a great deal, I allow;
But let us remember, before we deride,
   'Tis the nature, my dear, of a sow.

'But were a great boy, such as you, my dear Will,
   Like thèm to be eating all day,
Or be taking nice things till he made himself ill,
   What a glutton, indeed, we might say!

'If plum-cake and sugar he constantly picks,
   And sweetmeats, and comfits, and figs,
We should tell him to leave off his own greedy tricks,
   Before he finds fault with the pigs.'

23

Dirty Jack

There was one—little Jack—
Not so very long back,
And 'tis said to his lasting disgrace,
That he never was seen
With his hands at all clean,
And never quite clean was his face.

When to wash he was sent,
He sulkily went,
With water to splash himself o'er;
But he left the black streaks
All over his cheeks,
And made them look worse than before.

His friends were much hurt
To see so much dirt,
And often and well did they scour;
But all was in vain,
He was dirty again
Before they had done it an hour.

The pigs in the dirt
Could not be more expert
Than he was in grubbing about;
So at last people thought,
The young gentleman ought
To be made with four legs and a snout!

The Ragged Girl's Sunday

Mary Bennett

'Oh, dear Mamma, that little girl
    Forgets this is the day
When children should be clean and neat,
    And read, and learn, and pray!

'Her face is dirty and her frock,
  Holes in her stockings, see;
Her hair is such a fright, oh dear!
  How wicked she must be!

'She's playing in the kennel dirt
  With ragged girls and boys;
But *I* would not on Sunday touch
  My clean and pretty toys.

'*I* go to church, and sit so still,
  I in the garden walk,
Or take my stool beside the fire,
  And hear nice Sunday talk.

'*I* read my Bible, learn my hymns,
  My Catechism say;
That wicked little girl does not—
  She only cares to play!' . . .

Apple-pye

A Apple-pye! B bit it,
C cut it, D dealt it,
E eat it, F fought for it,
G got it, H had it,
J joined for it, K kept it,
L longed for it, M mourned for it,
N nodded at it, O opened it,
P peeped in it, Q quartered it,
R ran for it, S stole it,
T took it, U hewed it,
V viewed it, W wanted it;
X crossed it, Y yearned for it,
And Z put it in his pocket, and said,
    Well done! . . .

Says A, give me a good large slice.
Says B, a little Bit, but nice.
Says C, Cut me a piece of Crust.
Take it, says D, it's Dry as Dust.
Says E, I'll Eat it—fast who will.
Says F, I vow I'll have my Fill.
Says G, Gìve it me Good and Great.
Says H, a little bit I Hate.
Says I, *I* love the Juice the best,
And K the very same Confest.
Says L, there's nothing more I Love.
Says M, it Makes your teeth to Move.
N Noticed what the others said.
O Others' plates with grief surveyed.
P Praised the cook up to the life.
Q Quarrelled at so blunt a knife.
R was of Running short afraid.
S Silent Sat, and nothing Said.
T Thought that Talking might lose Time.
U Understoòd it at meàls a crìme.
W Wished that there had been a quince in;
Says X, these cooKS there's no convincing.
Says Y, Y'll eat, let others wish.
Z Sat as mute as any fish,
While Ampersy-and he licked the dish.

One-Two-Three

One—two—
Three—four—five:
I caught a hare alive:
Six—seven—
Eight—nine—ten:
I let her go again.

One, Two

One, two,
Buckle my shoe;
Three, four,
Knock at the door;
Five, six,
Pick up sticks;
Seven, eight,
Lay them straight;
Nine, ten,
A good fat hen.

Eleven, twelve,
Dig and delve;
Thirteen, fourteen,
Maids a-courting;
Fifteen, sixteen,
Maids a-kissing;
Seventeen, eighteen,
Maids a-waiting;
Nineteen, twenty,
My belly's empty.

Twenty-One

William Makepeace Thackeray

Oh, what fun!
A nice plum bun!
How I wish
It never was done!

27

A Counting-out Rhyme

Intery, mintery, cutery-corn,
Apple seed and apple thorn;
Wine, brier, limber-lock,
Five geese in a flock,
Sit and sing by a spring,
O-U-T, and in again.

The Vowels

Jonathan Swift

Wé are very little creatures,
All of different voice and features;
One of us in glAss is set,
One of us you'll find in jEt,
T'other you may see in tIn,
And the fourth a bOx within.
If the fifth you should pursue,
It can never fly from yoU.

Double-U

Heigh ho! my heart is low,
    My mind is all on one;
It's W for I know Who,
    And T for my love, Tom!

Mary and Her Kitten

Eleanor Farjeon

The Kitten's in the Dairy!
        Where's our Mary?
She isn't in the Kitchen,
She isn't at her Stitching,
She isn't at the Weeding,
        The Brewing, or the Kneading!
Mary's in the Garden, walking in a Dream,
Mary's got her Fancies, and the Kitten's got the Cream.

Bagpipes

A Cat came fiddling out of a barn,
With a pair of bagpipes under her arm;
Shè could sing nòthing but *fiddle cum fee*,
The mouse has married the humble bee.
Pipe Cat!   Dance Mouse!
We'll have a Wedding at our good house.

The Cat sat Asleep

The cat sat asleep by the fire,
The mistress snored loud as a pig,
Jack took up his fiddle by Jenny's desire
And struck up a bit of a jig.

The Three Cats

As I was going o'er misty moor
I spied three cats at a mill-door;
One was white and one was black,
And one was like my granny's cat.
I hopped o'er t'style and broke my heel,
I flew to Ireland very weel,
Spied an old woman sat by t'fire,
Sewing silk—jinking keys;
Cat's i' t'cream-pot up to t'knees;
Hen's i' t'hurdle crowing for day;
Cock's i' t'barn threshing corn—
I ne'er saw the like sin' I was born.

Bobby Shafto

Bobby Shafto's gone to sea,
Silver buckles at his knee;
He'll come back and marry me,
Bonny Bobby Shafto.

Bobby Shafto's bright and fair,
Combing down his yellow hair;
He's my ain for evermair,
Bonny Bobby Shafto.

Over the Water to Charley

Over the water, and over the sea,
And over the water to Charley;
Charley loves good ale and wine,
And Charley loves good brandy,
And Charley loves a pretty girl,
As sweet as sugar-candy.

Over the water, and over the sea,
And over the water to Charley;
I'll have none of your nasty beef,
Nor I'll have none of your barley;
But I'll have some of your very best flour,
To make a white cake for my Charley.

O, dear, O!

O, dear, O!
My cake's all dough,
And how to make it better
I *do not know*.

Five Very Old Riddles

Guess first, before you look at the answers on p. 204

There was a little green house—
And in the little green house
There was a little brown house,
And in the little brown house
There was a little yellow house,
And in the little yellow house
There was a little white house,
And in the little white house
There was a little heart.

A flock of white sheep
On a red hill;
Here they go, there they go,
Now they stand still!

As white as milk,
And not milk;
As green as grass,
And not grass;

As red as blood,
And not blood;
As black as soot,
And not soot!

I've seen you where you never was,
    And where you ne'er will be;
And yet you in that very same place
    May still be seen by me.

I had a little sister,
    They called her Pretty Peep;
She wades in the waters,
    Deep, deep, deep!
She climbs up the mountains,
    High, high, high;
My poor little sister
    She has but one eye.

The Spring Walk
Thomas Miller

We had a pleasant walk to-day,
Over the meadows and far away,
Across the bridge by the water-mill,
By the woodside, and up the hill;
And if you listen to what I say,
I'll tell you what we saw to-day. . . .

We saw upon the shady banks,
    Long rows of golden flowers shine,
And first mistook for buttercups,
    The star-shaped yellow celandine.

Anemones and primroses,
    And the blue violets of spring,
We found whilst listening by a hedge
    To hear a merry ploughman sing.

And from the earth the plough turned up
    There came a sweet refreshing smell,
Such as the lily of the vale
    Sends forth from many a woodland dell.

We saw the yellow wallflower wave
    Upon a mouldering castle wall,
And then we watched the busy rooks
    Among the ancient elm-trees tall.

And leaning from the old stone bridge,
    Below we saw our shadows lie,
And through the gloomy arches watched
    The swift and fearless swallows fly. . . .

Brother and Sister

William Wordsworth

. . . Oh! pleasant, pleasant were the days—
The time, when in our childish plays
My sister Emmeline and I
Together chased the butterfly!
A very hunter did I rush
Upon the prey: with leaps and springs
I followed on from brake to bush;
But she—God love her!—feared to brush
The dust from off its wings.

Mister Punchinello

Mother, I want to be married
To Mister Punchinello,
To Mister Punch, to Mister Chin, to Mister
    Nell, to Mister Lo,
    Pun—Chin—Nell—Lo—
To Mister Punchinello!

Secrets

Molly McArthur

Birds sang at twilight,
Down the dim street:
'Where are you going,
And whom will you meet?'

Back she called softly,
Clear as a bell:
'What do I care,
And why should I tell?

Where I go gaily,
Why gaily I go,
Everyone wonders:
No one shall know.'

Nanny

The moon shines bright,
The stars give light,
And little Nanny Button-cap
Will come to-morrow night.

Full Moon

Girls and boys, come out to play,
The moon is shining bright as day;
Leave your supper and leave your sleep,
And come with your play-fellows into the street;
Come with a *Whoop*, and come with a call,
Come with a good will, or come not at all.
Up the ladder and down the wall,
A half-penny roll will cover us all:
Yoù find milk and I'll find flour,
And we'll have a pudding in half-an-hour.

A Catching Song

for any Number of Players
Eleanor Farjeon

You càn't catch *me*!
You can't catch *me*!
Run as swift as quicksilver
You can't catch *me*!

If you can càtch me you shall have a ball
That ònce the dàughter of a kìng let fall;
It ran down the hill and it rolled on the plain,
And the kìng's daughter never caught her ball again,

And you can't catch *me*!
You can't catch *me*!
Run as quick as lightning,
But you can't catch *me*!

If you can catch me you shall have a bird
That once the son of a beggar heard.
He climbed up the tree, but the bird flew away,
And the bèggar's son never caught a bìrd thàt dày,

And you can't catch *me*!
You can't catch *me*!
Run as fast as water,
But you can't catch *me*!

The Garden Year

Sara Coleridge

January brings the snow,
Makes our feet and fingers glow.

February brings the rain,
Thaws the frozen lake again.

March brings breezes, loud and shrill,
To stir the dancing daffodil.

April brings the primrose sweet,
Scatters daisies at our feet.

May brings flocks of pretty lambs
Skipping by their fleecy dams.

June brings tulips, lilies, roses,
Fills the children's hands with posies.

Hot July brings cooling showers,
Apricots, and gillyflowers.

August brings the sheaves of corn,
Then the harvest home is borne.

Warm September brings the fruit;
Sportsmen then begin to shoot.

Fresh October brings the pheasant;
Then to gather nuts is pleasant.

Dull November brings the blast;
Then the leaves are whirling fast.

Chill December brings the sleet,
Blazing fire, and Christmas treat.

God, Our Maker

Mrs C. F. Alexander

All things bright and beautiful,
  All creatures great and small,
All things wise and wonderful,
  The Lord God made them all.

Each little flower that opens,
  Each little bird that sings,
He made their glowing colours,
  He made their tiny wings.

The purple-headed mountain,
  The river running by,
The sunset and the morning
  That brightens up the sky,

The cold wind in the winter,
  The pleasant summer sun,
The ripe fruits in the garden,
  He made them every one.

He gave us eyes to see them,
  And lips that we might tell
How great is God Almighty,
  Who has made all things well.

In March

William Wordsworth

The cock is crowing,
The stream is flowing,
The small birds twitter,
The lake doth glitter,
The green field sleeps in the sun:
  The oldest and youngest
  Are at work with the strongest:
The cattle are grazing,
Their heads never raising,
There are forty feeding like one! . . .

Hark!

Nòw chant Birds in every Bush,
The Blackbird and the speckled Thrush,
The pretty chirping Nightingale,
The Linnet, and the Waggletail,
The Mavis, and the Lark:
O how they do begin. . . . Hark! hark!

The Pretty Bird

Mary had a pretty bird
  With feathers bright and yellow—
Slender legs—upon my word—
  He *was* a pretty fellow.

'Coo'

The dove says, *Coo,*
  What shall I do?
It's hard, it's hard to keep my two.
  Pooh, says the wren,
  Why, I've got ten
And keep them all like gentlemen!

Nuts

The leaves are green, the nuts are brown,
They hang so high they will not come down;
Leave them alone till frosty weather,
Then they will all come down together.

Winter

Cold and raw the north wind doth blow,
  Bleak in the morning early;
All the hills are covered with snow,
  And winter's now come fairly.

A Warning

John Gay

Three children sliding on the ice
  Upon a summer's day,
It so fell out they all fell in;
  The rest they ran away.

Now, had these children been at home,
  Or sliding on dry ground,
Ten thousand pounds to one pen-*nee*
  They had not all been drowned!

You parents all that children have,
  And you that have got none,
If you would have them safe abroad,
  Pray keep them safe at home!

There's Snow on the Fields

Christina Rossetti

There's snow on the fields
  And cold in the cottage,
While I sit in the chimney nook
  Supping hot pottage.

My clothes are soft and warm,
   Fold upon fold,
But I'm so sorry for the poor
   Out in the cold.

Do as You'd be Done By

Little children, never give
Pain to things that feel and live;
Let the gentle robin come
For the crumbs you save at home—
As his food you throw along
He'll repay you with a song;
Never hurt the timid hare
Peeping from her green grass lair,
Let her come and sport and play
On the lawn at close of day;
The little lark goes soaring high
To the bright windows of the sky,
Singing as if 'twere always spring,
And fluttering on an untired wing—
Oh! let him sing his happy song,
Nor do these gentle creatures wrong.

Cock Robin

Cock Robin got up early
   At the breaking of the day,
He went to Jenny's window
   To sing a roundelay.

A roundelay of love he sang
   To pretty Jenny Wren,
And when he came unto the end
   Then he began again.

Jenny Wren fell sick,
    Upon a merry time,
In came Robin Redbreast
    And brought her sops in wine.

'Eat well of the sops, Jenny,
    Drink well of the wine.'
'Thank you, Robin, kindly,
    You shall be mine.'

Jenny she got well again
    And stood upon her feet.
She told Cock Robin plainly
    She loved him not a bit.

Robin being angry,
    He hopped upon a twig—
With, 'Out upon you! Fie upon you!
    Bold-faced jig!'

Who Killed Cock Robin?

Who killed Cock Robin?
    I, said the sparrow,
    With my bow and arrow,
I killed Cock Robin.

Who saw him die?
    I, said the fly,
    With my little eye,
And I saw him die.

Who catched his blood?
    I, said the fish,
    With my little dish,
And I catched his blood.

Who made his shroud?
    I, said the beadle,
    With my little needle,
And I made his shroud.

Who'll dig his grave?
    I, said the owl,
    With my spade and showl,
And I'll dig his grave.

Who'll be the parson?
    I, said the rook,
    With my little book,
And I'll be the parson.

Who'll be the clerk?
    I, said the lark,
    If 'tis not in the dark,
And I'll be the clerk.

Who'll carry him to the grave?
    I, said the kite,
    If 'tis not in the night,
And I'll carry him to his grave.

Who'll carry the link?
    I, said the linnet,
    I'll fetch it in a minute,
And I'll carry the link.

Who'll be chief mourner?
    I, said the dove,
    I mourn for my love,
And I'll be chief mourner.

Who'll bear the pall?
  We, said the wren,
  Both the cock and the hen,
And we'll bear the pall.

Who'll sing a psalm?
  I, said the thrush,
  As she sat in a bush,
And I'll sing a psalm.

And who'll toll the bell?
  I, said the bull,
  Because I can pull:
And so, Cock Robin, farewell!

All the birds in the air
  Fell to sighing and sobbing,
When they heard the bell toll
  For poor Cock Robin!

Bad Luck

The robin of the red breast,
  The robin and the wren;
If ye take out o' their nest,
  Ye'll never thrive again!

The robin of the redbreast,
  The martin and the swallow;
If ye touch one o' their eggs,
  Bad luck will surely follow!

43

The Babes in the Wood

My dear, do you know,
How a long time ago,
 Two poor little children
Whose names I don't know,
Were stolen away on a fine summer's day,
And left in a wood, as I've heard people say.

And when it was night,
So sad was their plight,
 The sun it went down,
And the moon gave no light.
They sobbed and they sighed, and they bitterly cried,
And the poor little things, they lay down and died.

And when they were dead,
The Robins so red
 Brought strawberry-leaves
And over them spread;
 And all the day long
 They sung them this song:
'Poor babes in the wood! Poor babes in the wood!
And don't you remember the babes in the wood?'

Rover and the Bird

Mrs Newton Crossland

. . . The crumbs from our breakfast [let's] scatter abroad,
 For the birds that fly wild in the air:
When the fruit-trees are bending beneath a rich load,
 We will not deny them their share.
If they do peck our peaches, and sometimes devour
 A cherry—ripe, ruddy, and sweet,
Remember the songs they so lavishly pour.
And you'll own that they merit the treat. . . .

Old Abram Brown

Old Abram Brown is dead and gone,
  You'll never see him more;
He used to wear a long brown coat,
  That buttoned down before.

There was a Man

There was a man, and he had nought,
  And robbers came to rob him;
He crept up into the chimney-pot,
  And then they thought they had him.

But he got down on t'other side,
  And then they could not find him.
He ran foùrteen miles in fifteen days,
  And never looked behind him.

And That's All

There was an old man,
And he had a calf,
    And that's half;
He took him out of the stall,
And put him on the wall,
    And that's all.

The Duke

The Duke of Cum-ber-land
  He had ten thousand men;
He marched them up to the top of the hill
  And he marched them down again.

When they were up, they were up,
  And when they were down, they were down,
And when they were only half-way up
  They were neither up nor down.

A Grace

Robert Herrick

Here a little child I stand,
Heaving up my either hand;
Cold as paddocks though they be,
Here I lift them up to Thee,
For a benison to fall
On our meat, and on us all. *Amen.*

James and the Shoulder of Mutton

Adelaide O'Keeffe

Young Jem at noon returned from school,
  As hungry as could be,
He cried to Sue, the servant-maid,
  'My dinner give to me.'

Said Sue, 'It is not yet come home;
  Besides, it is not late.'
'No matter that,' cries little Jem,
  'I do not like to wait.'

46

Quick to the baker's Jemmy went,
   And asked, 'Is dinner done?'
'It is,' replied the baker's man.
   'Then home I'll with it run.'

'Nay, Sir,' replied he prudently,
   'I tell you 'tis too hot,
And much too heavy 'tis for you.'
   '*I* tell you it is *not*.

'Papa, mamma, are both gone out,
   And I for dinner long;
So give it me, it is all mine,
   And, baker, hold your tongue.

'A shoulder 'tis of mutton nice!
   And batter-pudding too;
I'm glad of that, it is so good;
   How clever is our Sue!'

Now near the door young Jem was come,
   He round the corner turned,
But oh, sad fate! unlucky chance!
   The dish his fingers burned.

Low in the kennel down fell dish,
   And down fell all the meat:
Swift went the pudding in the stream,
   And sailed along the street.

The people laughed, and rude boys grinned
   At mutton's hapless fall;
But though ashamed, young Jemmy cried,
   'Better lose part than all.'

The shoulder by the knuckle he seized,
  His hands both grasped it fast,
And deaf to all their gibes and cries,
  He gained his home at last.

'Impatience is a fault,' cries Jem,
  'The baker told me true;
In future I will patient be,
  And mind what says our Sue.'

I saw a Ship

I saw a ship a-sailing,
A-sailing on the sea,
And oh, but it was laden
With pretty things for thee.

There were còmfits in the cabin,
And apples in the hold;
The sails were made of silk,
And the masts were made of gold.

The four and twenty sailors
That sat upon the deck,
Were four and twenty white mice
With chains about their necks.

The captain was a duck,
With a packet on his back;
And when the ship began to move,
The captain cried 'Quack! quack!'

Little Jack Horner

Jack Horner was a pretty lad,
   Near London he did dwell,
His father's heart he made full glad,
   His mother loved him well.
While little Jack was sweet and young,
   If he by chance should cry,
His mother pretty sonnets sung,
   With a *lul-la, lul-la-by*,
In such a dainty curious tone,
   As Jack sat on her knee,
So that, e'er he could go alone,
   He sang as well as she.

A pretty boy of curious wit,
   All people spoke his praise,
And in the corner would he sit
   In Christmas holydays.
When friends they did together meet,
   To pass away the time—
Why, little Jack, he sure would eat
   His Christmas pie in rhyme.
He'd sing, 'Jack Horner, in the corner,
   Eats good Christmas pie,
And with his thumbs pulls out the plumbs—
   A very good boy am I!'

The Elves' Dance

Round about, round about
    In a fair ring-a,
Thus we dance, thus we dance
    And thus we sing-a,
Trip and go, to and fro
    Over this green-a,
All about, in and out,
    For our brave Queen-a.

The Fairies

William Allingham

Up the airy mountain,
    Down the rushy glen,
We daren't go a-hunting,
    For fear of little men;
Wee folk, good folk,
    Trooping all together;
Green jacket, red cap,
    And white owl's feather!

Down along the rocky shore
    Some make their home,
They live on crispy pancakes
    Of yellow tide-foam;
Some in the reeds
    Of the black mountain-lake,
With frogs for their watch-dogs,
    All night awake.

High on the hill-top
  The old King sits;
He is now so old and gray
  He's nigh lost his wits.
With a bridge of white mist
  Columbkill he crosses,
On his stately journeys
  From Slieveleague to Rosses;
Or going up with music
  On cold starry nights,
To sup with the Queen
  Of the gay Northern Lights.

They stole little Bridget
  For seven years long;
When she came down again
  Her friends were all gone.
They took her lightly back,
  Between the night and morrow,
They thought that she was fast asleep,
  But she was dead with sorrow.
They have kept her ever since
  Deep within the lakes,
On a bed of flag-leaves,
  Watching till she wakes.

By the craggy hill-side,
  Through the mosses bare
They have planted thorn-trees
  For pleasure here and there.
Is any man so daring
  As dig one up in spite,
He shall find the thornies set
  In his bed at night.

Up the airy mountain,
   Down the rushy glen,
We daren't go a-hunting
   For fear of little men;
Wee folk, good folk,
   Trooping all together;
Green jacket, red cap,
   And white owl's feather!

To Bed

'Come, let's to bed,' says Sleepy-Head,
'Tarry awhile,' says Slow,
'Put on the pan,' says Greedy Nan,
'We'll sup before we go.'

Three a-Bed

He that lies at the stock,
Shall have the gold rock;
He that lies at the wall,
Shall have the gold ball;
He that lies in the middle,
Shall have the gold fiddle.

Now the Day is over

Sabine Baring-Gould

Now the day is over,
  Night is drawing nigh,
Shadows of the evening
  Steal across the sky.

Now the darkness gathers,
  Stars begin to peep,
Birds, and beasts, and flowers
  Soon will be asleep.

Jesu, give the weary
  Calm and sweet repose;
With Thy tenderest blessing
  May mine eyelids close.

Grant to little children
  Visions bright of Thee;
Guard the sailors tossing
  On the deep blue sea.

Comfort every sufferer
  Watching late in pain;
Those who plan some evil
  From their sin restrain.

Through the long night watches
  May Thine Angels spread
Their white wings above me,
  Watching round my bed.

When the morning wakens,
  Then may I arise
Pure, and fresh, and sinless
  In Thy Holy Eyes. . . .

Rockaby, Baby!

William Barnes

The rook's nest do rock on the tree-top
Where few foes can stand;
The martin's is high, and is deep
In the steep cliff of sand.
But thou, love, a-sleeping where footsteps
Must come to thy bed,
Hast father and mother to watch thee
And shelter thy head.
    Lullaby, Lilybrow. Lie asleep;
    Blest be thy rest.

And some birds do keep under roofen
Their young from the storm,
And some with nest-hoodings of moss
And of wool, do lie warm.
And we will look well to the house roof
That o'er thee might leak,
And the blast that might beat on thy window
Shall not smite thy cheek.
    Lullaby, Lilybrow. Lie asleep;
    Blest be thy rest.

Daybreak

H. W. Longfellow

A wind came up out of the sea,
And said, 'O mists, make room for me.'

It hailed the ships, and cried, 'Sail on,
Ye mariners, the night is gone;'

And hurried landward far away,
Crying, 'Awake! it is the day.'

It said unto the forest, 'Shout!
Hang all your leafy banners out!'

It touched the wood-bird's folded wing,
And said, 'O bird, awake and sing.'

And o'er the farms—'O chanticleer,
Your clarion blow, the day is near.'

It whispered to the fields of corn,
'Bow down, and hail the coming morn.'

It shouted through the belfry-tower,
'Awake, O bell! proclaim the hour.'

It crossed the churchyard with a sigh,
And said, 'Not yet! in quiet lie.'

The First Bee

From *The Snowdrop*
Mary Webb

. . . In the pale sunshine, with frail wings unfurled,
Comes to the bending snowdrop the first bee.
She gives her winter honey prudently;
And faint with travel in a bitter world,
The bee makes music, tentative and low,
And spring awakes and laughs across the snow.

Spring

Thomas Nash

Spring, the sweet Spring, is the year's pleasant king;
Then blooms each thing, then maids dance in a ring,
Cold doth not sting, the pretty birds do sing,
    Cuck-oo, jug-jug, pu-we, to-witta-woo!

The palm and may make country houses gay,
Lambs frisk and play, the shepherds pipe all day,
And we hear aye birds tune this merry lay,
　Cuck-oo, jug-jug, pu-we, to-witta-woo!

The fields breathe sweet, the daisies kiss our feet,
Young lovers meet, old wives a-sunning sit,
In every street these tunes our ears do greet,
　Cuck-oo, jug-jug, pu-we, to-witta-woo!
　　Spring! the sweet Spring!

Three Cuckoo Rhymes

I

Cuck-òo, Cuck-òo!
What do you do?
　'In April
I open my bill;
　In May
I sing night and day;
　In June
I change my tune;
　In July
Far—far I fly;
　In August
Away I *must*.'

II

The cuckoo he's a fine bird,
　He sings as he flies;
He brings us good tidings;
　He tells us no lies;

He sucks little birds' eggs
　To make his voice clear;
And when he sings *Cuck-oo!*
　The summer is near.

... Far in dark woods away
The lonely cuckoo hides,
With one soft word to say,
And not a note besides. ...

The Green Linnet

William Wordsworth

... Amid yon tuft of hazel trees,
That twinkle to the gusty breeze,
Behold him perched in ecstasies,
   Yet seeming still to hover;
There! where the flutter of his wings
Upon his back and body flings
Shadows and sunny glimmerings
   That cover him all over! ...

The Pet Lamb

William Wordsworth

The dew was falling fast, the stars began to blink;
I heard a voice: it said, 'Drink, pretty creature, drink!'
And, looking o'er the hedge, before me I espied
A snow-white mountain lamb, with a maiden at its side.

No other sheep were near, the lamb was all alone,
And by a slender cord was tethered to a stone;
With one knee on the grass did the little maiden kneel,
While to that mountain lamb she gave its evening meal.

The lamb, while from her hand he thus his supper took,
Seemed to feast with head and ears; and his tail with pleasure
   shook.
'Drink, pretty creature, drink,' she said, in such a tone
That I almost received her heart into my own. ...

The Swan

Translated from the Old English

My robe is noiseless while I tread the earth,
Or tarry 'neath the banks, or stir the shallows;
But when these shining wings, this depth of air,
Bear me aloft above the bending shores
Where men abide, and far the welkin's strength
Over the multitudes conveys me, then
With rushing whir and clear melodious sound
My raiment sings. And like a wandering spirit
I float unweariedly o'er flood and field.

Stupidity Street

Ralph Hodgson

I saw with open eyes
Singing birds sweet
Sold in the shops
For the people to eat,
Sold in the shops of
Stupidity Street.

I saw in vision
The worm in the wheat,
And in the shops nothing
For people to eat;
Nothing for sale in
Stupidity Street.

The Linnet

Robert Burns

Within the bush, her covert nest
A little linnet fondly prest;
The dew sat chilly on her breast,
    Sae early in the morning.

She soon shall see her tender brood,
The pride, the pleasure of the wood,
Amang the fresh green leaves bedewed
    Awake the early morning.

The Ant and the Cricket

A silly young cricket, accustomed to sing
Through the warm, sunny months of gay summer and
    spring,
Began to complain, when he found that at home
His cupboard was empty and winter was come.
    Not a crumb to be found
    On the snow-covered ground;
    Not a flower could he see,
    Not a leaf on a tree:
'Oh, what will become,' says the cricket, 'of me?'

At last by starvation and famine made bold,
All dripping with wet and all trembling with cold,
Away he set off to a miserly ant,
To see if, to keep him alive, he would grant
    Him shelter from rain:
    A mouthful of grain
    He wished only to borrow,
    He'd repay it to-morrow:
If not, he must die of starvation and sorrow.

Says the ant to the cricket, 'I'm your servant and friend,
But we ants never borrow, we ants never lend;
But tell me, dear sir, did you lay nothing by
When the weather was warm?' Said the cricket, 'Not I.
  My heart was so light
  That I sang day and night,
  For all nature looked gay.'
  'You *sang*, sir, you say?
Go then,' said the ant, 'and *dance* winter away!'

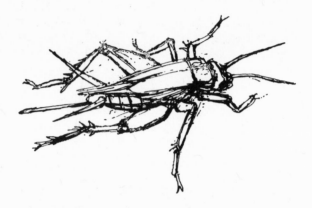

Thus ending, he hastily lifted the wicket
And out of the door turned the poor little cricket.
Though this is a fable, the moral is good:
If you live without work, you must live without food.

The Spider and the Fly

Mary Howitt

'Will you walk into my parlour?' said the Spider to the Fly;
''Tis the prettiest little parlour that ever you did spy;
The way into my parlour is up a winding stair,
And I have many curious things to show when you are there.'
'Oh *no, no*,' said the little Fly; 'to ask me is in vain;
For who goes up your winding stair can ne'er come down
  again.'

'I'm sure you must be weary, dear, with soaring up so high;
Will you rest upon my little bed?' said the Spider to the Fly.
'There are pretty curtains drawn around; the sheets are fine
    and thin;
And if you like to rest awhile, I'll snugly tuck you in!'
'Oh *no, no,*' said the little Fly; 'for I've often heard it said,
They never, never wake again who sleep upon your bed!'

Said the cunning Spider to the Fly: 'Dear friend, what can I
    do
To prove the warm affection I have *always* felt for you?
I have within my pantry good store of all that's nice;
I'm sure you're very welcome—will you please to take a
    slice?'
'Oh *no, no,*' said the little Fly; 'kind sir, that cannot be;
I've heard what's in your pantry, and I do not wish to see!'

'Sweet creature!' said the Spider, 'you are witty and you're
    wise;
How handsome are your gauzy wings, how brilliant are your
    eyes!
I have a little looking-glass upon my parlour shelf,
If you'll step in one mòment, dear, you shall behold yourself.'
'I thank you, gentle sir,' she said, 'for what you're pleased to
    say,
And bidding you good-morning now, I'll call another
    day. . . .'

For a Dewdrop

Eleanor Farjeon

Small shining drop, no lady's ring
Holds so beautiful a thing.
At sun-up in the early air
The sweetness of the world you snare.
Within your little mirror lie
The green grass and the wingèd fly,
The lowest flower, the tallest tree
In your crystal I can see,
Why, in your tiny globe you hold
The sun himself, a midge of gold!
It makes me wonder if the world
In which so many things are curled,
The world which all men real call,
Is not the real world at all,
But just a drop of dew instead
Swinging on a spider's thread.

Don't forget to make the 'real' in lines 13 and 14
just two syllables.

Precious Stones

Christina Rossetti

An emerald is as green as grass,
   A ruby red as blood,
A sapphire shines as blue as heaven,
   But a flint lies in the mud.

A diamond is a brilliant stone
   To catch the world's desire,
An opal holds a rainbow light,
   But a flint holds fire.

To make your Candles last for aye

To make your candles last for aye,
　　You wives and maids give ear—Oh!
To put 'em out's the only way,
　　Says honest John Boldèro.

The Child and the Snake

Mary Lamb

Henry was every morning fed
With a full mess of milk and bread.
One day the boy his breakfast took,
And ate it by a purling brook.
His mother lets him have his way,
With free leave Henry every day
Thither repairs, until she heard
Him talking of a fine *gray bird*.
This pretty bird, he said, indeed,
Came every day with him to feed;
And it loved hìm and loved his milk,
And it was smooth and soft like silk.

On the next morn she follows Harry,
And carefully she sees him carry
Through the long grass his heaped-up mess.
What was her terror and distress
When she saw the infant take
His bread and milk close to a snake!
Upon the grass he spreads his feast,
And sits down by his frightful guest,
Who had waited for the treat;
And now they both began to eat.

Fond mother! shriek not, O beware
The least small noise, O have a care—
The least small noise that may be made
The wily snake will be afraid—
If he hear the slightest sound,
He will inflict th'envenomed wound.
—She speaks not, moves not, scarce does breathe,
As she stands the trees beneath.
No sound she utters; and she soon
Seès the child lift up his spoon,
And tap the snake upon the head,
Fearless of harm; and then he said,
As speaking to familiar mate,
'Keep on your own side, do, Gray Pate!'
The snake then to the other side,
As one rebukèd, seems to glide;
And now again advancing nigh,
Again she hears the infant cry,
Tapping the snake, 'Keep farther, do;
Mind, Gray Pate, what I say to you!'

The danger's o'er! she sees the boy
(O what a change from fear to joy!)
Rise and bid the snake 'Good-bye.'
Says he, 'Our breakfast's done, and I
Will come again to-morrow day;'
—Then, lightly tripping, ran away.

Four-Paws

Helen Parry Eden

Four-Paws, the kitten from the farm,
  Is come to live with Betsy-Jane,
Leaving the stack-yard for the warm
  Flower-compassed cottage in the lane,
To wash his idle face and play
Among chintz cushions all the day.

Under the shadow of her hair
  He lies, who loves him nor desists
To praise his whiskers and compare
  The Tabby bracelets on his wrists—
Omelet at lunch and milk at tea
Suit Betsy-Jane and so fares he.

Happy beneath her golden hand
  He purrs contentedly nor hears
His mother mourning through the land—
  The old gray cat with tattered ears
And humble tail and heavy paw
Who brought him up among the straw.

Never by day she ventures nigh,
  But when the dusk grows dim and deep
And moths flit out of the strange sky
  And Betsy has been long asleep—
Out of the dark she comes and brings
Her dark maternal offerings;—

Some field-mouse or a throstle caught
  Near netted fruit or in the corn,
Or rat, for this her darling sought
  In the old barn where he was born;
And all lest on his dainty bed
Four-Paws were faint or under-fed.

Only between the twilight hours
 Under the window-panes she walks
Shrewdly among the scented flowers
 Nor snaps the soft nasturtium stalks,
Uttering still her plaintive cries,
And Four-Paws, from the house, replies,

Leaps from his cushion to the floor,
 Down the brick passage scantily lit,
Waits wailing at the outer door
 Till one arise and open it—
Then from the swinging lantern's light
Runs to his mother in the night.

The Irish Harper

Thomas Campbell

On the green banks of Shannon, when Sheelah was nigh,
No blithe Irish lad was so happy as I;
No harp like my own could so cheerily play,
And wherever I went was my poor dog Tray.

When at last I was forced from my Sheelah to part,
She said—while the sorrow was big at her heart:
'Oh! remember your Sheelah, when far, far away,
And be kind, my dear Pat, to our poor dog Tray.'

Poor dog! he was faithful, and kind, to be sure,
And he constantly loved me, although I was poor;
When the sour-looking folks sent me heartless away,
I had àlways a friend in my poor dog Tray.

When the road was so dark, and the night was so cold,
And Pat and his dog were grown weary and old,
How snugly we slept in my old coat of gray,
And he licked me for kindness—my poor dog Tray.

Though my wallet was scant, I remembered his case,
Nor refused my last crust to his pitiful face;
But he died at my feet one cold winter's day,
And I played a sad lament for my poor dog Tray.

Where now shall I go, poor, forsaken, and blind?
Can I find one to guide me, so faithful and kind?
To my sweet native village, so far, far away,
I can never more return with my poor dog Tray.

There was an Old Dog

A Game Rhyme

There was an old dog and he lived at the mill,
    And Bingo was his name, sir.
        B—I—N—G—O,
    And Bingo was his name, sir.

Bang her and bop her, and kick her and kop her,
    For Bingo was his name, sir.
Yòu sing, *bang her*, and I'll sing *bop her*,
    And you sing, *kick her*, and I'll sing, *kop her*,
And bang her and bop her, and kick her and kop her,
    And Bingo was his name, sir.

The miller he bought him a barrel of ale,
    And called it right good Stingo.
        S—T—I—N—G—O,
    And called it right good Stingo.
Chorus: Bang her . . .

The miller he went to town one day
  And bought a wedding-ring O.
    R—I—N—G—O,
  And bought a wedding-ring O.
Chorus: Bang her . . .

Now is not this a pretty tale?
  I swear it is by Jingo.
    J—I—N—G—O,
  I swear it is by Jingo.

Bang her and bop her, and kick her and kop her,
  For Bingo was his name, sir.
You sing, *bang her*, and I'll sing *bop her*,
  And you sing, *kick her*, and I'll sing, *kop her*,
And bang her and bop her, and kick her and kop her,
  And Bingo was his name, sir.

Lone Dog

Irene R. McLeod

I'm a lean dog, a keen dog, a wild dog, and lone;
I'm a rough dog, a tough dog, hunting on my own;
I'm a bad dog, a mad dog, teasing silly sheep;
I love to sit and bay the moon, to keep fat souls from sleep.

I'll never be a lap dog, licking dirty feet,
A sleek dog, a meek dog, cringing for my meat;
Not for me the fireside, the well-filled plate,
But shut door, and sharp stone, and cuff, and kick, and hate.

Not for me the other dogs, running by my side,
Some have run a short while, but none of them would bide;
O mine is still the lone trail, the hard trail, the best,
Wide wind, and wild stars, and the hunger of the quest!

The Woodman's Dog

William Cowper

Shaggy, and lean, and shrewd, with pointed ears
And tail cropped short, half lurcher and half cur—
His dog attends him. Close behind his heel
Now creeps he slow; and now, with many a frisk
Wide-scampering, snatches up the drifted snow
With ivory teeth, or ploughs it with his snout;
Then shakes his powdered coat, and barks for joy.

'Lauk a Mercy'

There was an old woman, as I've heard tell,
She went to market her eggs for to sell;
She went to market all on a market day.
And she fell asleep on the king's highway.

There came by a pedlar whose name was Stout,
He cut her petticoats all round about;
He cut her petticoats up to the knees,
Which made the old woman to shiver and freeze.

When this little woman first did wake,
She began to shiver and she began to shake,
She began to wonder and she began to cry,
'Lauk a mercy on me, this is none of I!

'But if it be I, as I do hope it be,
I've a little dog at home, and he'll know mè;
If it be I, he'll wag his little tail,
And if it be *not* I, he'll loudly bark and wail!'

Hòme went the little woman all in the dark,
Up got the little dog, and he began to bark;
He began to bark, so she began to cry,
'Lauk a mercy on me, this *can't* be I!'

As I walked

As I walked by myself,
And talked to myself,
    Myself said unto me,
Look to thyself,
Take care of thyself,
    For nobody cares for thee.

I answered myself,
And said to myself,
    In the self-same repartee,
Look to thyself,
Or not look to thyself,
    The self-same thing will be.

There was a Lady

There was a lady loved a swine,
  'Honey,' quoth she,
'Pig-Hog, wilt thou be mine?'—
  Hunc, quoth he.

'I'll build for thee a silver sty,
    Honey,' quoth she;
'And there in comfort thou shalt lie.'
    Hunc, quoth he.

'It shall be pinned with a silver pin,
    Honey,' quoth she;
'For latch when you go out and in.'
    Hunc, quoth he.

'Oh tell me then when we shall wed,
    Honey?' quoth she.
Hunc, hunc, *HUNC*, he said,
    And away went he.

A Tragic Story
William Makepeace Thackeray

There lived a sage in days of yore,
And he a handsome pigtail wore;
But wondered much and sorrowed more,
    Because it hung behind him.

He mused upon this curious case,
And swore he'd change the pigtail's place,
And have it hanging at his face,
    Not dangling there behind him.

Says he, 'The mystery I've found,—
I'll turn me round,'—he turned him round;
    But still it hung behind him.

Then round and round, and out and in,
All day the puzzled sage did spin;
In vain—it mattered not a pin—
    The pigtail hung behind him.

71

And right, and left, and round about,
And up, and down, and in, and out
He turned; but still the pigtail stout
  Hung steadily behind him.

And though his efforts never slack,
And though he twist, and twirl, and tack,
Alas! still faithful to his back,
  The pigtail hangs behind him.

A Man of Words

A man of words and not of deeds,
Is like a garden full of weeds;
And when the weeds begin to grow,
It's like a garden full of snow;
And when the snow begins to fall,
It's like a bird upon the wall;
And when the bird away does fly,
It's like an eagle in the sky;
And when the sky begins to roar,
It's like a lion at the door;
And when the door begins to crack,
It's like a stick across your back;
And when your back begins to smart,
It's like a penknife in your heart;
And when your heart begins to bleed,
You're dead, and dead, and dead, indeed.

Yer's Tu Thee

To be sung in Devon round an apple-tree in Spring

Yer's tü thee, old apple-tree,
Be zure yü bud, be zure yü blaw,
And bring voth apples gude enow,
    Hats vul! Caps vul!
Dree-bushel bags vul,
Pockets vul and awl!
    Urrah! Urrah!
Aw 'ess, hats vul, caps vul,
And dree-bushel bags vul,
    Urrah! Urrah!

Calm

Michael Drayton

The wind had no more strength than this
   —That leisurely it blew—
To make one leaf the next to kiss
   That closely by it grew. . . .

Signs of Rain

Edward Jenner

The hollow winds begin to blow,
The clouds look black, the glass is low,
The soot falls down, the spaniels sleep,
The spiders from their cobwebs peep;
Last night the sun went pale to bed,
The moon in haloes hid her head;
The boding shepherd heaves a sigh,
For, see, a rainbow spans the sky:
The walls are damp, the ditches smell,
Closed is the pink-eyed pimpernel.
Hark how the chairs and tables crack!
Old Betty's joints are on the rack;

73

Loud quack the ducks, the peacocks cry,
The distant hills are seeming nigh.
How restless are the snorting swine;
The busy flies disturb the kine;
Low o'er the grass the swallow wings,
The cricket, too, how sharp he sings;
Puss on the hearth, with velvet paws,
Sits wiping o'er her whiskered jaws.
Through the clear stream the fishes rise,
And nimbly catch the incautious flies.
The glow-worms, numerous and bright,
Illumed the dewy dell last night.
At dusk the squalid toad was seen,
Hopping and crawling o'er the green;
The whirling wind the dust obeys,
And in the rapid eddy plays;
The frog has changed his yellow vest,
And in a russet coat is dressed.
Though June, the air is cold and still,
The mellow blackbird's voice is shrill.
My dog, so altered in his taste,
Quits mutton-bones on grass to feast;
And see yon rooks, how odd their flight,
They imitate the gliding kite,
And seem precipitate to fall,
As if they felt the piercing ball.
'Twill surely rain I see with sorrow,
Our jaunt must be put off to-morrow.

The Kite

Adelaide O'Keeffe

My Kite is three feet broad, and six feet long;
The standard straight, the bender tough and strong,
And to its milk-white breast five painted stars belong.

Grand and majestic soars my paper kite,
  Through trackless skies it takes its lofty flight.
Nor lark nor eagle flies to such a noble height.

  As in the field I stand and hold the twine,
  Swift I unwind, to give it length of line,
Yet swifter it ascends, nor will to earth incline.

  Like a small spèck, so high I see it sail,
  I hear its pinions flutter in the gale,
And, like a flock of wild geèse, sweeps its flowing tail.

A Boy's Song

James Hogg

Where the pools are bright and deep,
Where the gray trout lies asleep,
Up the river and o'er the lea,
That's the way for Billy and me.

Where the blackbird sings the latest,
Where the hawthorn blooms the sweetest,
Where the nestlings chirp and flee,
That's the way for Billy and me.

Where the mowers mow the cleanest,
Where the hay lies thick and greenest,
There to trace the homeward bee,
That's the way for Billy and me.

Where the hazel bank is steepest,
Where the shadow falls the deepest,
Where the clustering nuts fall free,
That's the way for Billy and me. . . .

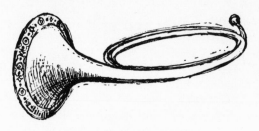

The Hunt is up

The hunt is up, the hunt is up,
　　And it is well-nigh day;
And Harry our king is gone hunting
　　To bring his deer to bay.

The east is bright with morning light,
　　And darkness it is fled;
And the merry horn wakes up the morn
　　To leave his idle bed.

Behold the skies with golden dyes
　　Are glowing all around;
The grass is green, and so are the treen
　　All laughing at the sound.

The horses snort to be at sport,
　　The dogs are running free,
The woods rejoice at the merry noise
　　Of *Hey tantara tee ree!*

The sun is glad to see us clad
　　All in our lusty green,
And smiles in the sky as he riseth high
　　To see and to be seen.

Awake all men, I say again,
　　Be merry as you may;
For Harry our king is gone hunting,
　　To bring his deer to bay.

A-hunting we will go

Henry Fielding

The dusky night rides down the sky,
   And ushers in the morn;
The hounds all join in glorious cry,
   The huntsman winds his horn.
     And a-hunting we will go.

The wife around her husband throws
   Her arms to make him stay:
'My dear, it rains, it hails, it blows;
   You cannot hunt to-day.'
     Yet a-hunting we will go.

Away they fly to escape the rout,
   Their steeds they soundly switch;
Some are thrown in, and some thrown out,
   And some thrown in the ditch.
     Yet a-hunting we will go.

Sly Reynard now like lightning flies,
   And sweeps across the vale;
And when the hounds too near he spies,
   He drops his bushy tail.
     Then a-hunting we will go.

Fond echo seems to like the sport,
   And join the jovial cry;
The woods, the hills, the sound retort,
   And music fills the sky,
     When a-hunting we do go.

At last his strength to faintness worn,
    Poor Reynard ceases flight;
Then, hungry, homeward we return.
    To feast away the night,
        And a-drinking we do go.

Ye jovial hunters in the morn
    Prepare then for the chase;
Rise at the sounding of the horn,
    And health with sport embrace
        When a-hunting we do go.

Ee-oh!

The fox and his wife they had a great strife,
They never eat mustard in all their whole life,
They eat their meat without fork or knife,
    And lov'd to be picking a bone, *ee-oh!*

The fox jumped up on a moonlight night;
The stars they were shining, and all things bright
'Oh, ho!' said the fox, 'it's a very fine night,
    For me to go through the town, *ee-oh!*'

The fox, when he came to yonder stile,
He lifted his lugs and he listened a while!
'Oh, ho!' said the fox, 'it's a very short mile
    From this unto yonder wee town, *ee-oh!*'

The fox when he came to the farmer's gate,
Who should he see but the farmer's drake;
'I love you well for your master's sake,
    And long to be picking your bone, *ee-oh!*'

The grey goose she ran round the farmer's stack,
'Oh, ho!' said the fox, 'you are plump and fat;
You'll grease my beard and ride on my back,
    From this into yonder wee town, *ee-oh!*'

The farmer's wife she jumped out of bed,
And out of the window she popped her head!
'Oh, husband! oh, husband! The geese are all dead,
    For the fox has been through the town, *ee-oh!*'

The farmer he loaded his pistol with lead,
And shot the old rogue of a fox through the head;
'Ah, ha!' said the farmer, 'I think you're quite dead;
    And no more you'll trouble the town, *ee-oh!*'

The Lincolnshire Poacher

When I was bound apprentice in famous Lincolnshire,
Full well I served my master for more than seven year,
Till I took up to poaching—as you shall quickly hear;
    Oh, 'tis my delight on a shining night
    In the season of the year!

As me and my comrade were setting of a snare,
'Twas then we spied the gamekeeper, for him we did not
        care,
For we can wrestle and fight, my boys, and jump o'er
        anywhere:
    Oh, 'tis my delight on a shining night
    In the season of the year!

As me and my comrade were setting four or five,
And taking on 'em up again we caught a hare alive,
We took the hare alive, my boys, and through the woods
        did steer:
    Oh, 'tis my delight on a shining night
    In the season of the year!

I threw him on my shoulder, and then we all trudged home,
We took him to a neighbour's house and sold him for a
    crown,
We sold him for a crown, my boys, but I did not tell you
    where;
    Oh, 'tis my delight on a shining night
    In the season of the year!

Success to every gentleman that lives in Lincolnshire,
Success to every poacher that wants to sell a hare,
Bad luck to every gamekeeper that will not sell his deer:
    Oh, 'tis my delight on a shining night
    In the season of the year!

THREE OWL RHYMES

The White Owl

Lord Tennyson

When cats run home and light is come,
    And dew is cold upon the ground,
And the far-off stream is dumb,
    And the whirring sail goes round,
    And the whirring sail goes round;
      Alone and warming his five wits,
      The white owl in the belfry sits.

When merry milkmaids click the latch,
    And rarely smells the new-mown hay,
And the cock hath sung beneath the thatch
    Twice or thrice his roundelay,
    Twice or thrice his roundelay;
      Alone and warming his five wits,
      The white owl in the belfry sits.

Once I was a Monarch's Daughter

Once I was a monarch's daughter,
   And sat on a lady's knee;
But am now a nightly rover,
   Banished to the ivy tree.
Crying *hoo, hoo, hoo, hoo, hoo, hoo,*
   Hoo, hoo, hoo, my feet are cold.
Pity me, for here you see me
   Persecuted, poor, and old.

The Barn Owl

Samuel Butler

While moonlight, silvering all the walls,
Through every mouldering crevice falls,
Tipping with white his powdery plume,
As shades or shifts the changing gloom;
The Owl that, watching in the barn,
Sees the mouse creeping in the corn,
Sits still and shuts his round blue eyes
As if he slept—until he spies
The little beast within his stretch—
Then starts—and seizes on the wretch!

The Sound of a Gun

From *Autumn*
Ann Taylor

... But hark! from the woodlands the sound of a gun,
 The wounded bird flutters and dies;
Where can be the pleasure, for nothing but fun,
 To shoot the poor thing as it flies? ...

When Reynard at midnight steals down to the farm,
 And kills the poor chickens and cocks;
Then rise, Father Goodman, there can be no harm
 In chasing a thief of a fox.

Or you, Mr. Butcher, and Fisherman, you
 May follow your trades, I must own:
So chimneys are swept, when they want it—but who
 Would sweep them for pleasure alone?

If men would but think of the torture they give
 To creatures that cannot complain,
They surely would let the poor animals live,
 And not make a sport of their pain!

The Bells of Heaven

Ralph Hodgson

'Twould ring the bells of Heaven
The wildest peal for years,
If Parson lost his senses
And people came to theirs,
And he and they together
Knelt down with angry prayers
For tamed and shabby tigers
And dancing dogs and bears,
And wretched, blind pit-ponies,
And little hunted hares.

The Old Friar Remembers

Thomas Love Peacock

Though I be now a grey, grey friar,
Yet I was once a hale young knight,
The cry of my dogs was the only quoir
In which my spirit did take delight.

Little I recked of matin bell,
But drowned its toll with my clanging horn,
And the only beads I loved to tell,
Were the beads of dew on the spangled thorn.

Elegy Written in a Country Churchyard

Thomas Gray

The curfew tolls the knell of parting day,
  The lowing herd wind slowly o'er the lea,
The ploughman homeward plods his weary way,
  And leaves the world to darkness and to me.

Now fades the glimmering landscape on the sight,
  And all the air a solemn stillness holds,
Save where the beetle wheels his droning flight,
  And drowsy tinklings lull the distant folds:

Save that, from yonder ivy-mantled tower,
  The moping owl does to the moon complain
Of such as, wandering near her secret bower,
  Molest her ancient solitary reign. . . .

A Cradle Song

Lord Tennyson

Sweet and low, sweet and low,
    Wind of the western sea,
Low, low, breathe and blow,
    Wind of the western sea!
Over the rolling waters go,
Come from the dying moon, and blow,
    Blow him again to me;
While my little one, while my pretty one, sleeps.

Sleep and rest, sleep and rest,
    Father will come to thee soon;
Rest, rest, on mother's breast,
    Father will come to thee soon;
Father will come to his babe in the nest,
Silver sails all out of the west
    Under the silver moon:
Sleep, my little one, sleep, my pretty one, sleep.

O Lady Moon

Christina Rossetti

O Lady Moon, your hòrns point to the East;
    Shine, be increased!
O Lady Moon, your horns point to the West;
    Wane, be at rest!

The New Moon

William Cullen Bryant

When, as the garish day is done,
Heaven burns with the descended sun,
  'Tis passing sweet to mark,
Amid the flush of crimson light,
The new moon's modest bow grow bright,
  As earth and sky grow dark. . . .

Lucy Gray, or Solitude

William Wordsworth

Oft I had heard of Lucy Gray:
  And, when I crossed the wild,
I chanced to see, at break of day,
  The solitary child.

No mate, no comrade Lucy knew;
  She dwelt on a wide moor,
The sweetest thing that ever grew
  Beside a human door!

You yet may spy the fawn at play,
  The hare upon the green;
But the sweet face of Lucy Gray
  Will never more be seen.

'To-night will be a stormy night,
  You to the town must go;
And take a lantern, Child, to light
  Your mother through the snow.'

'That, Father, will I gladly do:
  'Tis scarcely afternoon,
The minster-clock has just struck two,
  And yonder is the moon!'

At this the Father raised his hook,
  And snapped a fagot-brand.
He plied his work; and Lucy took
  The lantern in her hand.

Not blither is the mountain roe:
  With many a wanton stroke
Her feet disperse the powdery snow,
  That rises up like smoke.

The storm came on before its time:
  She wandered up and down:
And many a hill did Lucy climb:
  But never reached the town.

The wretched parents all that night
  Went shouting far and wide;
But there was neither sound nor sight
  To serve them for a guide.

At daybreak on the hill they stood
  That overlooked the moor;
And thence they saw the bridge of wood,
  A furlong from their door.

They wept—and, turning homeward, cried,
  'In heaven we all shall meet;'
When in the snow the mother spied
  The print of Lucy's feet.

Then downwards from the steep hill's edge
  They tracked the footmarks small;
And through the broken hawthorn-hedge,
  And by the low stone-wall;

And then an open field they crossed—
  The marks were still the same—
They tracked them on, nor ever lost;
  And to the bridge they came.

They followed from the snowy bank
  Those footmarks, one by one,
Into the middle of the plank;
  And further there were none!

—Yet some maintain that to this day
  She is a living child;
That you may see sweet Lucy Gray
  Upon the lonesome wild.

O'er rough and smooth she trips along,
  And never looks behind;
And sings a solitary song
  That whistles in the wind.

Dark

From *Angels in the Air*
S. W. Partridge

Dark, darker grew the leaden sky,
  The wind was moaning low,
And, shrouding all the herbless ground,
  Sad, silently, and slow,
Wending from heaven its weary way
  Fell the white flaked snow. . . .

My Playmate

James Greenleaf Whittier

The pines were dark on Ramoth hill,
　Their song was soft and low;
The blossoms in the sweet May wind
　Were falling like the snow.

The blossoms drifted at our feet,
　The orchard birds sang clear;
The sweetest and the saddest day
　It seemed of all the year.

For—more to me than birds or flowers—
　My playmate left her home,
And took with her the laughing spring,
　The music and the bloom.

She kissed the lips of kith and kin,
　She laid her hand in mine:
What more could ask the bashful boy
　Who fed her father's kine?

She left us in the bloom of May:
　The constant years told o'er
Their seasons with as sweet May morns,
　But she came back no more. . . .

The wild grapes wait us by the brook,
　The brown nuts on the hill,
And still the May-day flowers make sweet
　The woods of Follymill.

The lilies blossom in the pond,
　The bird builds in the tree,
The dark pines sing on Ramoth hill
　The slow song of the sea.

I wonder if she thinks of them,
    And how the old time seems,
If ever the pines of Ramoth wood
    Are sounding in her dreams.

I see her face, I hear her voice:
    Does she remember mine?
And what to her is now the boy
    Who fed her father's kine?

What cares she that the orioles build
    For other eyes than ours,
That other laps with nuts are filled,
    And other hands with flowers? . . .

Nurse's Song

William Blake

When the voices of children are heard on the green,
And laughing is heard on the hill,
My heart is at rest within my breast,
And everything else is still.

'Then come home, my children, the sun is gone
        down,
And the dews of night arise;
Come, come, leave off play, and let us away
Till the morning appears in the skies.'

'No, no, let us play, for it is yet day,
And we cànnot go to sleep;
Besides, in the sky the little birds fly,
And the hills are all covered with sheep.

'Well, well, go and play till the light fades away,
And then go home to bed.'
The little ones leaped and shouted and laughed
And all the hills echoèd.

Bed in Summer

Robert Louis Stevenson

In winter I get up at night
And dress by yellow candle-light.
In summer, quite the other way,
I have to go to bed by day.

I have to go to bed and see
The birds still hopping on the tree,
Or hear the grown-up people's feet
Still going past me in the street.

And does it not seem hard to you,
When all the sky is clear and blue,
And I should like so much to play,
To have to go to bed by day?

Song

H. W. Longfellow

Stay, stay at home, my heart, and rest;
Home-keeping hearts are happiest,
For those that wander they know not where
Are full of trouble and full of care;
    To stay at home is best. . . .

Up in the Morning early

Robert Burns

Up in the morning's no for me,
   Up in the morning early:
When a' the hills are covered wi' snaw,
   I'm sure it's winter fairly.

Cauld blaws the wind frae east to west,
   The drift is driving sairly;
Sae loud and shrill's I hear the blast,
   I'm sure it's winter fairly.

The birds sit chittering in the thorn,
   A' day they fare but sparely;
And lang's the night frae e'en to morn;
   I'm sure it's winter fairly.

Winter Streams

Bliss Carman

Now the little rivers go
Muffled safely under snow,

And the winding meadow streams
Murmur in their wintry dreams,

While a tinkling music wells
Faintly from their icy bells. . . .

Wul 'e plaize

Wul 'e plaize tü remimber
  Tha veefth ov Novimber
Tha gunpowder trayson an' plot;
  I daunt zee no rayson
  Why gunpowder trayson
Shüde iver be vurgot.
    Guy Fawkes, Guy!
He and 'is companions dìd contrive
Tü blaw all Englan' up alive,
With a dark lantern an' a match,
By God's massy 'e wuz catched.
    Guy Fawkes, Guy!

Wassail Song

Here we come a-wassailing
  Among the leaves so green,
Here we come a-wandering,
  So fair to be seen. . . .

We are not daily beggars
  That beg from door to door,
But we are neighbours' children
  Whom you have seen before. . . .

God bless the master of this house,
  Likewise the mistress too;
And all the little children
  That round the table go. . . .

And all your kin and kinsfolk,
  That dwell both far and near;
We wish you a Merry Christmas,
  And a happy New Year.

Oranges

Dingty, diddledy, my mammy's maid,
  She *stole* oranges, I am afraid,
Some in her pocket, some in her sleeve,
  She stole oranges, I do believe.

The Bag Pudding

When good King Arthur ruled this land,
  He was a goodly king;
He stole three pecks of barley-meal,
  To màke a bàg-puddìng.

A bag-pudding the Queen did make,
  And stuffed it full of plums;
And in it put great lumps of fat,
  As big as my two thumbs.

The King himself did eat thereof,
  And noblemen beside;
And what they could not eat that night
  The Queen next morning fried.

The Story of Augustus, who would not have any Soup

Heinrich Hoffman

Augustus was a chubby lad;
Fat, ruddy cheeks Augustus had;
And everybody saw with joy
The plump and hearty, healthy boy.
He ate and drank as he was told,
And never let his soup get cold.

But one day—one cold winter's day,
He screamed out—'Tàke the soup away!
Oh take the nasty soup awày!
I *won't* have any soup to-day.'

Next day begins his tale of woes;
Quite lank and lean Augustus grows.
Yet, though he feels so weak and ill,
The naughty fellow cries out still—
'Not any soup for me, I say:
Oh take the nasty soup away!
I *won't* have any soup to-day.'

The third day comes: Oh what a sin!
To make himself so pale and thin.
Yet, when the soup is put on table,
He screams, as loud as he is able,
'Not any soup for me, I say:
Oh take the nasty soup away!
I-won't-have-any-soup-to-day.'

Look at him, now the fourth day's come!
He scarcely weighs a sugar-plum;
He's like a little bit of thread,
And on the fifth day, he was—dead!

Beautiful Soup

Lewis Carroll

Beautiful Soup, so rich and green,
Waiting in a hot tureen!
Who for such dainties would not stoop?
Soup of the evening, beautiful Soup!
Soup of the evening, beautiful Soup!
    Beau—ootiful Soo—oop!
    Beau—ootiful Soo—oop!
Soo—oop of the e—e—evening,
    Beautiful, beautiful Soup!

Beautiful Soup! Who cares for fish,
Game, or any other dish?
Who would not give all else for two p–
   ennyworth only of beautiful Soup?
Pennyworth only of beautiful Soup?
    Beau—ootiful Soo—oop!
    Beau—ootiful Soo—oop!
Soo—oop of the e—e—evening,
    Beau–ti–ful, beauti—FUL SOUP!

The Walrus and the Carpenter

Lewis Carroll

The sun was shining on the sea,
   Shining with all his might:
He did his very best to make
   The billows smooth and bright—
And this was odd, because it was
   The middle of the night.

The moon was shining sulkily,
    Because she thought the sun
Had got no business to be there
    After the day was done—
'It's very rude of him,' she said,
    'To come and spoil the fun!'

The sea was wet as wet could be,
    The sands were dry as dry.
You could not see a cloud, because
    No cloud was in the sky:
No birds were flying overhead—
    There were no birds to fly.

The Walrus and the Carpenter
    Were walking close at hand;
They wept like anything to see
    Such quantities of sand:
'If this were only cleared away,'
    They said, 'it *would* be grand!'

'If seven maids with seven mops
    Swept it for half a year,
Do you suppose,' the Walrus said,
    'That they could get it clear?'
'I doubt it,' said the Carpenter,
    And shed a bitter tear.

'O Oysters, come and walk with us!'
    The Walrus did beseech.
'A pleasant walk, a pleasant talk,
    Along the briny beach:
We cannot do with more than four,
    To give a hand to each.'

The eldest Oyster looked at him,
  But never a word he said:
The eldest Oyster winked his eye,
  And shook his heavy head—
Meaning to say he did not choose
  To leave the oyster-bed.

But four young Oysters hurried up,
  All eager for the treat:
Their coats were brushed, their faces washed,
  Their shoes were clean and neat—
And this was odd, because, you know,
  They hadn't any feet.

Four other Oysters followed them,
  And yet another four;
And thick and fast they came at last,
  And more, and more, and more—
All hopping through the frothy waves,
  And scrambling to the shore.

The Walrus and the Carpenter
  Walked on a mile or so,
And then they rested on a rock
  Conveniently low:
And all the little Oysters stood
  And waited in a row.

'The time has come,' the Walrus said,
  'To talk of many things:
Of shoes—and ships—and sealing-wax—
  Of cabbages—and kings—
And why the sea is boiling hot—
  And whether pigs have wings.'

'But wait a bit,' the Oysters cried,
  'Before we have our chat;
For some of us are out of breath,
  And all of us are fat!'
'No hurry!' said the Carpenter.
  They thanked him much for that.

'A loaf of bread,' the Walrus said,
  'Is what we chiefly need:
Pepper and vinegar besides
  Are very good indeed—
Now if you're ready, Oysters dear,
  We can begin to feed.'

'But not on us!' the Oysters cried,
  Turning a little blue.
'After such kindness, that would be
  A dismal thing to do!'
'The night is fine,' the Walrus said.
  'Do you admire the view?

'It was so kind of you to come!
  And you are very nice!'
The Carpenter said nothing but
  'Cut us another slice:
I wish you were not quite so deaf—
  I've had to ask you twice!'

'It seems a shame,' the Walrus said,
  'To play them such a trick,
After we've brought them out so far,
  And made them trot so quick!'
The Carpenter said nothing but
  'The butter's spread too thick.'

'I weep for you,' the Walrus said:
    'I deeply sympathise.'
With sobs and tears he sorted out
    Those of the largest size,
Holding his pocket-handkerchief
    Before his streaming eyes.

'O Oysters,' said the Carpenter,
    'You've had a pleasant run!
Shall we be trotting home again?'
    But answer there was none—
And this was scarcely odd, because
    They'd eaten every one.

The Dessert

Mary Lamb

With the apples and the plums
Little Carolina comes,
At the time of the dessèrt she
Comes and drops her new last curtsy;
Graceful curtsy, practised o'er
In the nursery before.
Whàt shall we compare her to?
The dessèrt itsèlf will do.
Like preserves she's kept with care,
Like blanched almonds she is fair,
Soft as down on peach her hair,
And so soft, so smooth is each
Pretty cheek as that same peach,
Yet more like in hue to cherries;
Then her lips—the sweet strawberries—
Caroline herself shall try them
If they are not like when nigh them;
Her bright eyes are black as sloes,
But I think we've none of those

Common fruit here—and her chin
From a round point does begin,
Like the small end of a pear;
Whiter drapery she does wear
Than the frost on cake; and sweeter
Than the cake itself, and neater,
Though bedecked with emblems fine,
Is our little Caroline.

I remember

Thomas Hood

I remember, I remember
The house where I was born,
The little window where the sun
Came peeping in at morn;
He never came a wink too soon,
Nor brought too long a day;
But now I often wish the night
Had borne my breath away!

I remember, I remember
The roses, red and white,
The violets and the lily-cups,
Those flowers made of light!
The lilacs where the robin built,
And where my brother set
The laburnum on his birthday,
The tree is living yet!

I remember, I remember,
Where I was used to swing,
And thought the air must rush as fresh
To swallows on the wing;

My spirit flew in feathers then,
That is so heavy now,
And summer pools could hardly cool
The fever on my brow!

I remember, I remember,
The fir-trees dark and high;
I used to think their slender tops
Were close against the sky:
It was a childish ignorance,
But now 'tis little joy
To know I'm farther off from heaven
Than when I was a boy.

Tom at Dinner

(In the old spelling)

Adelaide O'Keeffe

One day little Tom in his clean pin-afore,
   Was seated at table, and dinner served in;
Though Tom was not helped, yet with patience he bore
   Whilst every one round him was wagging a chin.

They laughed, eat, and drank, with a hearty good cheer,
   The hot smoaking dishes looked tempting and nice;
Still Tom was forgot, tho' his hunger severe
   Now wanted no dainties his wish to entice.

At length, to his father, with voice soft and sweet,
   'I'll thank you,' said he, 'for some salt, if you please.'
'Some salt!'—'Yes,' said Tom, 'when you give me some meat,
   'My salt I'll have ready—I don't wish to *teaze*.'

All present was struck with his patience and wit,
   His mother caressed him with kisses so kind,
His father then gave him the choicest tit-bit:
   Thus Tommy got praises and jovially dined.

A True Story

Ann Taylor

Little Ann and her mother were walking one day
   Through London's wide city so fair,
And business obliged them to go by the way
   That led them through Cavendish Square.

And as they passed by the great house of a Lord,
   A beautiful chariot there came,
To take some most elegant ladies abroad,
   Who straightway got into the same.

The ladies in feathers and jewels were seen,
   The chariot was painted all o'er,
The footmen behind were in silver and green,
   The horses were prancing before.

Little Ann by her mother walked silent and sad,
   A tear trickled down from her eye,
Till her mother said, 'Ann, I should be very glad
   To know what it is makes you cry.'

'Mamma,' said the child, 'see that carriage so fair,
   All covered with varnish and gold,
Those ladies are riding so charmingly there,
   While we have to walk in the cold.

'You say God is kind to the folks that are good,
   But surely it cannot be true;
Or else I am certain, almost, that He would
   Give such a fine carriage to you!'

'Look there, little girl,' said her mother, 'and see
   What stands at that very coach door;
A poor ragged beggar, and listen how she
   A halfpenny tries to implore.

'All pale is her face, and deep sunk is her eye,
    Her hands look like skeleton's bones;
She has got a few rags, just about her to tie,
    And her naked feet bleed on the stones.'

'Dear ladies,' she cries, and the tears trickle down,
    'Relieve a poor beggar, I pray;
I've wandered all hungry about this wide town,
    And not ate a morsel to-day.

'My father and mother are long ago dead,
    My brother sails over the sea,
And I've scarcely a rag, or a morsel of bread,
    As plainly, I'm sure, you may see.

'A fever I caught, which was terribly bad,
    But no nurse or physic had I;
An old dirty shed was the house that I had,
    And only on straw could I lie.

'And now that I'm better, yet feeble and faint,
    And famished, and naked, and cold,
I wander about with my grievous complaint,
    And seldom get aught but a scold.

'Some will not attend to my pitiful call,
    Some think me a vagabond cheat;
And scarcely a creature relieves me, of all
    The thousands that traverse the street.

'Then ladies, dear ladies, your pity bestow——'
    Just then a tall footman came round,
And asking the ladies which way they would go,
    The chariot turned off with a bound.

'Ah! see, little girl,' then her mother replied,
  'How foolish those murmurs have been;
You have but to look on the contrary side,
  To learn both your folly and sin.

'This poor little beggar is hungry and cold,
  No mother awaits her return;
And while such an object as this you behold,
  Your heart should with gratitude burn.

'Your house and its comforts, your food and your
      friends,
  'Tis favour in God to confer;
Have you any claim to the bounty He sends,
  Who makes you to differ from her?

'A coach, and a footman, and gaudy attire,
  Give little true joy to the breast;
To be good is the thing you should chiefly desire,
  And then leave to God all the rest.'

O Sweet Content!

Thomas Dekker

Art thou poor, and hast thou golden slumbers?
    O sweet content!
Art thou rich, and is thy mind perplexed?
    O punishment!
Dost thou laugh to see how fools are vexed
To add to golden numbers, golden numbers?
O sweet content! O sweet, O sweet content!
  Work apace, apace, apace, apace;
  Honest labour bears a lovely face;
Then *hey nonny nonny, hey nonny nonny!* . . .

O Happy!

O happy who thus liveth,
   Not caring much for gold;
With clothing, which sufficeth
   To keep him from the cold:—
Though poor and plain his diet,
Yet merry it is and quiet.

Alice Fell

William Wordsworth

The post-boy drove with fierce career,
For threatening clouds the moon had drowned;
When, as we hurried on, my ear
Was smitten with a startling sound.

As if the wind blew many ways,
I heard the sound—and more and more;
It seemed to follow with the chaise,
And still I heard it as before.

At length I to the boy called out;
He stopped his horses at the word,
But neither cry, nor voice, nor shout,
Nor aught else like it, could be heard.

The boy then smacked his whip, and fast
The horses scampered through the rain;
But hearing soon upon the blast
The cry, I bade him halt again.

Forthwith alighting on the ground,
'Whence comes,' said I, 'this piteous moan?'
And there a little girl I found,
Sitting behind the chaise alone.

'My cloak!' no other word she spake,
But loud and bitterly she wept,
As if her innocent heart would break;
And down from off her seat she leapt.

'What ails you, child?'—She sobbed, 'Look here!'
I saw it in the wheel entangled,
A weather-beaten rag as e'er
From any garden scarecrow dangled.

There, twisted between nave and spoke,
It hung, nor could at once be freed;
But our joint pains unloosed the cloak,
A miserable rag indeed!

'And whither are you going, child,
To-night, along these lonesome ways?'
'To Durham,' answered she, half wild.
'Then come with me into the chaise.'

Insensible to all relief
Sat the poor girl, and forth did send
Sob after sob, as if her grief
Could never, never have an end.

'My child, in Durham do you dwell?'
She checked herself in her distress,
And said, 'My name is Alice Fell;
I'm fatherless and motherless.

'And I to Durham, Sir, belong.'
Again, as if the thought would choke
Her very heart, her grief grew strong;
And all was for her tattered cloak.

The chaise drove on; our journey's end
Was nigh; and, sitting by my side,
As if she had lost her only friend,
She wept, nor would be pacified.

Up to the tavern-door we post;
Of Alice and her grief I told,
And I gave money to the host,
To buy a new cloak for the old.

'And let it be of duffil gray,
As warm a cloak as man can sell!'
—Pròud creature wàs she the next day,
The little orphan, Alice Fell!

The Chimney Sweeper
William Blake

When my mother died I was very young,
And my father sold me while yet my tongue
Could scarcely cry, *'weep! 'weep! 'weep! 'weep!*
So your chimneys I sweep, and in soot I sleep.

There's little Tom Dacre, who cried when his head,
That curl'd like a lamb's back, was shaved; so I said,
'Hush, Tom! never mind it, for when your head's bare,
You know that the soot cannot spoil your white hair.'

And so he was quiet: and that very night,
As Tom was a-sleeping, he had such a sight,
That thousands of sweepers, Dick, Joe, Ned, and Jack,
Were all of them locked up in coffins of black.

And by came an angel, who had a bright key,
And he opened the coffins, and set them all free;
Then down a green plain, leaping, laughing they run,
And wash in a river, and shine in the sun.

Then naked and white, all their bags left behind,
They rise upon clouds, and sport in the wind;
And the angel told Tom, if he'd be a good boy,
He'd have God for his father, and never want joy.

And so Tom awoke; and we rose in the dark,
And got with our bags and our brushes to work;
Though the morning was cold, Tom was happy and warm:
So, if all do their duty, they need not fear harm.

The Reverie of Poor Susan
William Wordsworth

At the corner of Wood Street, when daylight appears,
Hangs a thrush that sings loud, it has sung for three years:
Poor Susan has passed by the spot, and has heard
In the silence of morning the song of the bird.

'Tis a note of enchantment; what ails her? She sees
A mountain ascending, a vision of trees;
Bright volumes of vapour through Lothbury glide,
And a river flows on through the vale of Cheapside.

Green pastures she views in the midst of the dale,
Down which she so often has tripped with her pail;
And a single small cottage, a nest like a dove's,
The one only dwelling on earth that she loves.

She looks, and her heart is in heaven: but they fade,
The mist and the river, the hill and the shade:
The stream will not flow, and the hill will not rise,
And the colours have all passed away from her eyes!

Jock O' Hazeldean

Sir Walter Scott

'Why weep ye by the tide, ladye?
  Why weep ye by the tide?
I'll wed you to my youngest son,
  And ye shall be his bride.
And ye shall be his bride, ladye,
  Sae comely to be seen!'
But aye she loot the tears doon fa'
  For Jock o' Hazeldean.

'Now let this wilfu' grief be done,
  And dry that cheek so pale:
Young Frank is chief of Errington,
  And lord of Langley-dale;
His step is first in peaceful ha',
  His sword in battle keen,'
But aye she loot the tears doon fa'
  For Jock o' Hazeldean.

'A chain of gold ye shall not lack,
  Nor braid to bind your hair;
Nor mettled hound, nor managed hawk,
  Nor palfrey fresh and fair:
And you, the foremost o' them a',
  Shall ride our forest queen'—
But aye she loot the tears doon fa'
  For Jock o' Hazeldean.

The kirk was decked at morning-tide,
  The tapers glimmered fair;
The priest and bridegroom wait the bride,
  And dame and knight were there.
They sought her baith by bower and ha';
  The lady was not seen:
She's o'er the border and awa'
  Wi' Jock o' Hazeldean!

The Sailor's Wife

W. J. Mickle

And are ye sure the news is true?
   And are ye sure he's weel?
Is this a time to think o' wark?
   Ye jades, lay by your wheel;
Is this the time to spin a thread,
   When Colin's at the door?
Reach down my cloak, I'll to the quay,
   And see him come ashore.

   For there's nae luck about the house,
      There's nae luck at a';
   There's little pleasure in the house
      When our gudeman's awa'.

And gie to me my bigonet,
   My bishop's satin gown;
For I maun tell the bailie's wife
   That Colin's in the town.
My Turkey slippers maun gae on,
   My stockin's pearly blue;
It's a' to pleasure our gudeman,
   For he's baith leal and true.

Rise, lass, and mak a clean fireside,
   Put on the muckle pot;
Gie little Kate her button gown
   And Jock his Sunday coat;
And mak their shoon as black as slaes,
   Their hose as white as snaw;
It's a' to please my ain gudeman,
   For he's been long awa'.

There's twa fat hens upo' the coop
    Been fed this month and mair;
Mak haste and thraw their necks about,
    That Colin weel may fare;
And spread the table neat and clean,
    Gar ilka thing look braw,
For wha can tell how Colin fared
    When he was far awa'?

Sae true his heart, sae smooth his speech,
    His breath like caller air;
His very foot has music in't
    As he comes up the stair:—
And will I see his face again?
    And will I hear him speak?
I'm downright dizzy wi' the thought,
    In troth I'm like to greet.

If Colin's weel, and weel content,
    I hae nae mair to crave,
And gin I live to keep him sae,
    I'm blest aboon the lave:
And will I see his face again,
    And will I hear him speak?
I'm downright dizzy wi' the thought,
    In troth I'm like to greet.

    For there's nae luck about the house,
        There's nae luck at a';
    There's little pleasure in the house
        When our gudeman's awa'.

The Piper

William Blake

Piping down the valleys wild,
Piping songs of pleasant glee,
On a cloud I saw a child,
And he laughing said to me:

'Pipe a song about a Lamb!'
So I piped with merry cheer.
'Piper, pipe that song again;'
So I piped: he wept to hear.

'Drop thy pipe, thy happy pipe;
Sing thy songs of happy cheer:'
So I sang the same again,
While he wept with joy to hear.

'Piper, sit thee down and write
In a book, that all may read.'
So he vanished from my sight,
And I plucked a hollow reed,

And I made a rural pen,
And I stained the water clear,
And I wrote my happy songs
Every child may joy to hear.

Fairy Song

John Lyly

By the moon we sport and play,
With the night begins our day;
As we dance the dew doth fall;
Trip it, little urchins all!
Lightly as the wingèd bee,
Two by two, and three by three,
And about go we, and about go we!

Over Hill, over Dale

William Shakespeare

Over hill, over dale,
  Thorough bush, thorough brier,
Over park, over pale,
  Thorough flood, thorough fire,
I do wander every where,
Swifter than the moones sphere;
And I serve the fairy queen,
To dew her orbs upon the green:
The cowslips tall her pensioners be;
In their gòld coats spots you see;
Those be rubies, fairy favours,
In their freckles live their savours:
I must go seek some dew-drops here,
And hang a pearl in every cowslip's ear.

Evening Song

John Fletcher

Shepherds all, and maidens fair,
Fold your flocks up, for the air
'Gins to thicken, and the sun
Already his great course hath run.
See the dew-drops how they kiss
Every little flower that is,
Hanging on their velvet heads,
Like a rope of crystal beads: ..

113

The Holly and the Ivy

The holly and the ivy,
Now both are full well grown—
Of all the trees that are in the wood,
The holly bears the crown:

Oh, the rising of the sun,
The running of the deer,
The playing of the merry organ,
Sweet singing in the choir.

The holly bears a blossom,
As white as lily-flower,
And Mary bore sweet Jesus Christ
To be our sweet Saviour:

The holly bears a berry,
As red as any blood,
And Mary bore sweet Jesus Christ
To do poor sinners good:

The holly bears a prickle,
As sharp as any thorn,
And Mary bore sweet Jesus Christ
On Christmas day in the morn:

The holly bears a bark,
As bitter as any gall,
And Mary bore sweet Jesus Christ
For to redeem us all:

The holly and the ivy,
Now both are full well grown—
Of all the trees that are in the wood,
The holly bears the crown:

    Oh, the rising of the sun,
    The running of the deer,
    The playing of the merry organ,
    Sweet singing in the choir.

A New Year Carol

Here we bring new water
    from the well so clear,
For to worship God with,
    this happy New Year.

Sing *levy dew*, sing *levy dew*,
    the water and the wine;
The seven bright gold wires
    and the bugles that do shine.

Sing reign of Fair Maid,
    with gold upon her toe,
Open you the West Door,
    and turn the Old Year go.

Sing reign of Fair Maid
    with gold upon her chin,
Open you the East Door,
    And let the New Year in.

Sing *levy dew*, sing *levy dew*,
    the water and the wine;
The seven bright gold wires
    and the bugles they do shine.

Let us with a Gladsome Mind

John Milton

Let us with a gladsome mind
Praise the Lord, for He is kind,
For His mercies shall endure,
Ever faithful, ever sure.

All our wants He doth supply,
Loves to hear our humble cry,
For His mercies shall endure,
Ever faithful, ever sure.

All things living He doth feed,
His full hand supplies their need,
For His mercies shall endure,
Ever faithful, ever sure.

Merry are the Bells and merry would they ring

Merry are the bells, and merry would they ring;
Merry was myself, and merry could I sing;
With a merry ding-dong, happy, gay, and free,
And a merry sing-song, happy let us be!

Waddle goes your gait, and hollow are your hose;
Noddle goes your pate, and purple is your nose;
Merry is your sing-song, happy, gay, and free,
With a merry ding-dong, happy let us be!

Merry have we met, and merry have we been;
Merry let us part, and merry meet again;
With our merry sing-song, happy, gay, and free,
And a merry ding-dong, happy let us be!

Dance!

Dance, thumbkin, dance,
Dance, thumbkin, dance;
Dance, ye merry men all around:
But thumbkin he can dance alone;
But thumbkin he can dance alone.

Dance, foreman, dance,
Dance, foreman, dance;
Dance, ye merry men all around:
But thumbkin he can dance alone;
But thumbkin he can dance alone.

Dance, middleman, dance, *etc.*

Dance, ringman, dance, *etc.*

Dance, littleman, dance, *etc.*

Bo Peeper

Bo Peeper,
Nose dreeper,
Chin chopper,
White lopper,
Red rag,
And little gap.

Here Sits

Here sits the lord mayor,
  Here his two men;
Here sits the cock,
  Here sits the hen;
Here sit the little chickens,
  Here they run in;
Chinchopper, chinchopper,
  Chinchopper, chin!

The Silly

My daddy is dead, and I can't tell you how;
He left me six horses to follow the plough:
  With my *Whim, wham, waddle, oh!*
  Strim, stram, straddle, oh!
  Blowsey boys, bubble, oh,
  Over the brow!

I sold my six horses and bought me a cow;
To make me a fortune though I didn't know how:
  With my *Whim, wham* . . .

I sold my old cow and bought me a calf,
For I never made bargain but lost the best half:
  With my *Whim, wham* . . .

I bartered my calf and I bought me a cat,
To sit at the fire and to warm her small back:
  With my *Whim, wham* . . .

I sold my small cat and bought me a mouse,
And with flame in his tail he burnt down my house:
  With my *Whim, wham, waddle, oh!*
  Strim, stram, straddle, oh!
  Blowsey boys, bubble, oh,
  Over the brow!

The Priest and the Mulberry-Tree

Thomas Love Peacock

Did you hear of the curate who mounted his mare,
And merrily trotted along to the fair?
Of creature more tractable none ever heard;
In the height of her speed she would stop at a word;
But again with a word, when the curate said, 'Hey!'
She put forth her mettle and galloped away.

As near to the gates of the city he rode,
While the sun of September all brilliantly glowed,
The good priest discovered, with eyes of desire,
A mulberry-tree in a hedge of wild brier;
On boughs long and lofty, in many a green shoot,
Hung large, black, and glossy, the beautiful fruit.

The curate was hungry and thirsty to boot;
He shrunk from the thorns, though he longed for the
    fruit;
With a word he arrested his courser's keen speed,
And he stood up erect on the back of his steed;
On the saddle he stood while the creature stood still,
And he gathered the fruit till he took his good fill.

'Sure never,' he thought, 'was a creature so rare,
So docile, so true, as my excellent mare;
Lo, here now I stand,' and he gazed all around,
'As safe and as steady as if on the ground;
Yet how had it been, if some traveller this way,
Had, dreaming no mischief, but chanced to cry,
    "Hey"?'

He stood with his head in the mulberry-tree,
And he spoke out aloud in his fond reverie.
At the sound of the word the good mare made a push,
And down went the priest in the wild-brier bush,
He remembered too late, on his thorny green bed,
MUCH THAT WELL MAY BE THOUGHT CANNOT
    WISELY BE SAID.

The Boys and the Apple-Tree

Adelaide O'Keeffe

As William and Thomas were walking one day,
   They came by a fine orchard's side:
They would rather eat apples than spell, read, or play,
   And Thomas to William then cried:

'O brother, look yonder! what clusters hang there!
   I'll try and climb over the wall:
I must have an apple; I will have a pear;
   Although it should cost me a fall!'

Said William to Thomas, 'To steal is a sin,
   Mamma has oft told this to thee:
I never have stole, nor will I begin,
   So the apples may hang on the tree.'

'You are a good boy, as you ever have been,'
   Said Thomas, 'let's walk on, my lad:
We'll call on our schoolfellow, Benjamin Green,
   Who to see us, I know, will be glad.'

They came to the house, and asked at the gate,
  'Is Benjamin Green now at home?'
But Benjamin did not allow them to wait,
  And brought them both into the room.

And he smiled, and he laughed, and capered with joy,
  His little companions to greet:
'And we too are happy,' said each little boy,
  'Our playfellow dear thus to meet.'

'Come, walk in our garden, this morning so fine,
  We may, for my father gives leave;
And more, he invites you to stay here and dine;
  And a most happy day we shall have!'

But when in the garden, they found 'twas the same
  They saw as they walked in the road;
And near the high wall, when those little boys came,
  They started, as if from a toad:

'That large ring of iron, you see on the ground,
  With terrible teeth like a saw,'
Said their friend, 'the guard of our garden is found,
  And it keeps all intruders in awe.

'If any the warning without set at nought,
  Their legs then this man-trap must tear.'
Said William to Thomas, 'So you'd have been caught
  If you had leaped over just there.'

Cried Thomas, in terror of what now he saw,
  'With my faults I will heartily grapple;
For I learn what may happen by breaking a law,
  Although but in stealing an apple.'

The True Story of Web-Spinner

Mary Howitt

Web-spinner was a miser old,
  Who came of low degree;
His body was large, his legs were thin,
  And he kept bad company;
And his visage had the evil look
  Of a black felon grim;
To all the country he was known,
  But none spoke well of him.
His house was seven stories high,
  In a corner of the street,
And it always had a dirty look,
  When other homes were neat;
Up in his garret dark he lived,
  And from the windows high,
Looked oùt in the dusky evening
  Upon the passers by.
Most people thought he lived alone,
  Yet many have averred
That dismal cries from out his house
  Were often loudly heard;
And that none living left his gate,
  Although a few went in;
For he seized the very beggar old,
  And stripped him to the skin.
And though he prayed for mercy,
  Yet mercy ne'er was shown—
The miser cut his body up,
  And picked him bone from bone.
Thus people said, and all believed
  The dismal story true;
As it was told to me, in truth,
  I tell it so to you.

There was an ancient widow—
  One Madgy de la Moth,
A stranger to the man, or she
  Had ne'er gone there in troth:
But she was poor and wandered out,
  At night-fall in the street,
To beg from rich men's tables
  Dry scraps of broken meat.
So she knocked at old Web-Spinner's door
  With a modest tap, and low,
And down stairs came he speedily
  Like an arrow from a bow.
'Walk in, walk in, mòther,' said he,
  And shut the door behind—
She thought, for such a gentleman,
  That he was wondrous kind.
But ere the midnight clock had tolled,
  Like a tiger of the wood
He had eaten the flesh from off her bones,
  And drunk of her heart's blood!

Now after this foul deed was done,
  A little season's space,
The burly Baron of Bluebottle
  Was riding from the chase.
The sport was dull, the day was hot,
  The sun was sinking down,
When wearily the Baron rode
  Into the dusty town.

Says he, 'I'll ask a lodging,
 At the first hoùse I come tò;'
With that, the gate of Web-Spinner
 Came suddenly in view;
Loud was the knock the Baron gave:
 Down came the churl with glee;
Says Bluebottle, 'Good Sir, to-night
 I ask your courtesy;
I am wearied by a long day's chase—
 My friends are far behind.'
'You may need them all,' said Web-Spinner,
 'It runneth in my mind.'
'A Baron am I,' said Bluebottle;
 'From a foreign land I come;'
'I thought as much,' said Web-Spinner,
 'Fools never stay at home!'
Says the Baron, 'Churl, what meaneth this?
 I defy you, villain base!'
And he wished the while, in his inmost heart,
 He was safely from the place.
Web-Spinner ran and locked the door,
 And a loud laùgh laughed he,
With that, each one on the other sprang,
 And they wrestled furiously.
The Baron was a man of might,
 A swordsman of renown;
But the Miser had the stronger arm,
 And kept the Baron down.
Then out he took a little cord,
 From a pocket at his side,
And with many a crafty, cruel knot,
 His hands and feet he tied;
And bound him down unto the floor,
 And said in savage jest,
'There is heavy work for you in store;
 So, Baron, take your rest!'

Then up and down his house he went,
　Arranging dish and platter,
With a dull and heavy countenance,
　As if nothing were the matter.
At length he seized on Bluebottle,
　That strong and burly man,
And, with many and many a desperate tug,
　To hoist him up began:
And step by step and step by step,
　He went with heavy tread;
But ere he reached the garret door,
　Poor Bluebottle was dead.

Now all this while, a magistrate,
　Who lived in a house hard by,
Had watched Web-Spinner's cruelty
　Through a window privily:
So in he burst, through bolts and bars,
　With a loud and thundering sound,
And vowed to burn the house with fire,
　And level it with the ground;
But the wicked churl, who all his life
　Had looked for such a day,
Passed through a trap-door in the wall,
　And took himself away.
But where he went, no man could tell:
　'Twas said that under ground
He died a miserable death—
　But his body ne'er was found.
They pulled his house down, stick and stone,
　'For a caitiff vile as he,'
Said they, 'within our quiet town
　Shall not a dweller be!'

Little Billee

William Makepeace Thackeray

There were three sailors of Bristol city
Who took a boat and went to sea.
But first with beef and captain's biscuits
And pickled pork they loaded she.

There was gorging Jack and guzzling Jimmy,
And the youngest he was little Bill-ee.
Now when they got as far as the Equator
They'd nothing left but one split pea.

Says gorging Jack to guzzling Jimmy,
'I am extremely hungaree.'
To gorging Jack says guzzling Jimmy,
'We've nothing left, we must eat we.'

Says gorging Jack to guzzling Jimmy,
'With one another we shouldn't agree!
There's little Bill, he's young and tender,
We're old and tough, so let's eat he.

'Oh, Billy, we're going to kill and eat you,
So undo the button of your chemie.'
When Bill received this information
He used his pocket handkerchie.

'First let me say my catechism,
Which my poor mammy taught to me.'
'Make haste, make haste,' says guzzling Jimmy,
While Jack pulled out his snickersnee.

So Billy went up to the main-top gallant mast,
And down he fell on his bended knee.
He scarce had come to the twelfth commandment
When up he jumps. 'There's land I see:

'Jerusalem and Madagascar,
And North and South Amerikee:
There's the British flag a-riding at anchor,
With Admiral Napier, K.C.B.'

So when they got aboard of the Admiral's,
He hanged fat Jack and flogged Jimmee:
But as for little Bill he made him
The Captain of a Seventy-three.

Sailor and Tailor

A sailor lad and a tailor lad,
   And they were baith for me;
I wid raither tak the sailor lad,
   And lat the tailor be.

What can a tailor laddie dee
   But sit and sew a cloot?
But the bonnie sailor laddie—*he*
   Can turn the ship aboot.

He can turn her east, he can turn her west,
   He can turn her far awa';
He aye tells me t'keep up my hairt
   For the time that he's awa'.

I saw 'im lower his anchor,
   I saw 'im as he sailed;
I saw 'im cast his jacket
   To try and catch a whale.

He skips upon the planestanes,
  He sails upon the sea;
A fancy man wi' a curly pow
  Is aye the boy for me,
  Is aye the boy for me;
A fancy man wi' a curly pow
  Is aye the boy for me.

He daurna brack a biscuit,
  He daurna smoke a pipe;
He daurna kiss a bonnie lass
  At ten o'clock at night.

I can wash a sailor's shirt,
  And I can wash it clean;
I can wash a sailor's shirt,
  And bleach it on the green.

Come *a-rinkle-tinkle*,
  Come *a-rinkle-tin*,
With *a-fal-lal-la*, and *a-fal-lal-lor*
  Aboun a man-o'-war.

The Sailor's Consolation
Charles Dibdin

One night came on a hurricane,
  The sea was mountains rolling,
When Barney Buntline slewed his quid
  And said to Billy Bowline:
'A strong nor'-wester's blowing, Bill:
  Hark! don't ye hear it roar now?
Lord help 'em, how I pities them
  Unhappy folks on shore now.

'Foolhardy chaps as live in towns,
    What danger they are all in,
And now lie quaking in their beds,
    For fear the roof should fall in!
Poor creatures, how they envies us
    And wishes, I've a notion,
For our good luck in such a storm
    To be upon the ocean!

'And as for them that's out all day
    On business from their houses,
And late at night returning home
    To cheer their babes and spouses;
While you and I, Bill, on the deck
    Are comfortably lying,
My eyes! what tiles and chimney-pots
    About their heads are flying!

'Both you and I have oft-times heard
    How men are killed and undone
By overturns from carriages,
    By thieves and fires, in London.
We know what risks these landsmen run,
    From noblemen to tailors;
Then, Bill, let us thank Providence
    That you and I are sailors.'

Black-eyed Susan
John Gay

All in the Downs the fleet was moored,
    The streamers waving in the wind,
When black-eyed Susan came aboard.
    'Oh! where shall I my true love find?
Tèll me, ye jovial sailors, tell me true,
If my sweet William sails among the crew.'

William, who high upon the yard
    Rocked with the billow to and fro,
Soon as her well-known voice he heard,
    He sighed, and cast his eyes below:
The cord slides swiftly through his glowing hands,
And (quick as lightning) on the deck he stands.

So the sweet lark, high poised in air,
    Shuts close his pinions to his breast,
If chance his mate's shrill call he hear,
    And drops at once into her nest:—
The noblest captain in the British fleet
Might envy William's lip those kisses sweet. . . .

On a Friday Morn

On a Friday morn, as we set sail,
    It was not far from land,
O there I spy'd a pretty, fair maid,
    With a comb and a glass in her hand.

        And the stormy winds did blow,
            And the raging seas did roar,
        And while wè jolly sailor-boys were up into the
            top,
            The land-lubbers laid them down below,
                below, below—
        And the land-lubbers laid them down below.

Then up spoke a boy of our gallant ship,
    And a well-speaking boy was he:
'My father and my mother they live in Portsmouth
    town,
    And to-night they will weep for me.'

Then up spoke a man of our gallant ship,
    And a well-speaking man was he:
'I have a fair wife up in London town,
    And to-night she a widow will be.'

Then up spoke the captain of our gallant ship,
    And a valiant man was he:
'For the want of a boat we shall all be drowned,
    For she's sunk to the bottom of the sea.'

The moon shone bright, and the stars gave light,
    And my mother was looking for me;
She may look and weep with watery eyes—
    She may look to the bottom of the sea.

Three times round went our gallant ship,
    Full three times round went she;
Three times roùnd and roùnd she went,
    Then she sunk to the bottom of the sea.

        And the stormy winds did blow,
            And the raging seas did roar,
        And while we jolly sailor-boys were up into the top,
            The land-lubbers laid them down below, below,
                below—
            And the land-lubbers laid them down below.

The Ancient Mariner

Samuel Taylor Coleridge

'The moving Moon went up the sky,
    And nowhere did abide;
Softly she was going up,
    And a star or two beside—

'Her beams bemocked the sultry main,
    Like April hoar-frost spread;
But where the ship's huge shadow lay,
    The charmèd water burnt alway
    A still and awful red.

'Beyond the shadow of the ship,
I watched the water-snakes:
They moved in tracks of shining white.
And when they reared, the elfish light
Fell off in hoary flakes.

'Within the shadow of the ship
I watched their rich attire:
Blue, glossy green, and velvet black,
They coiled and swam; and every track
Was a flash of golden fire.

'O happy living things! no tongue
Their beauty might declare:
A spring of love gushed from my heart,
And I blessed them unaware:
Sure my kind saint took pity on me,
And I blessed them unaware. . . .'

.   .   .   .

'Around, around, flew each sweet sound,
Then darted to the Sun;
Slowly the sounds came back again,
Now mixed, now one by one.

'Sometimes a-dropping from the sky
I heard the skylark sing;
Sometimes all little birds that are,
How they seemed to fill the sea and air
With their sweet jargoning!

'And now 'twas like all instruments,
Now like a lonely flute;
And now it is an angel's song,
That makes the Heavens be mute.

'It ceased: yet still the sails made on
A pleasant noise till noon,
A noise like of a hidden brook
In the leafy month of June,
That to the sleeping woods all night
Singeth a quiet tune. . . .'

The Ship

Sir John Squire

There was no song nor shout of joy
   Nor beam of moon or sun,
When she came back from the voyage
   Long ago begun;
But twilight on the waters
   Was quiet and gray,
And she glided steady, steady and pensive,
   Over the open bay.

Her sails were brown and ragged,
   And her crew hollow-eyed,
But their silent lips spoke content
   And their shoulders pride;
Though she had no captives on her deck,
   And in her hold
There were no heaps of corn or timber
   Or silks or gold.

The 'Shannon' and the 'Chesapeake'

On board the *Shannon* frigate,
    In the merry month of May,
To watch those bold Americans,
    Off Boston lights we lay.
The *Chesapeake* was in harbour,
    A frigate stout and fine—
Four hundred and forty men had she,
    Her guns were forty-nine.

'Twas Captain Broke commanded us—
    A challenge he did write
To the captain of the *Chesapeake*,
    To bring her out to fight:
Our captain says—'Brave Lawrence,
    'Tis not from enmity;
But 'tis to prove to all the world
    That we do rule the sea.

'Don't think, my noble captain,
    Because you've had success,
That British tars are humbled—
    Not even in distress.
No! we will fight like heroes,
    Our glory to maintain,
In defiance of your greater size
    And the number of your men.'

That challenge was accepted;
    The Americans came down—
A finer frigate ne'er belonged
    Unto the British crown.
They brought her into action,
    On our true English plan;
Nor fired a shot till within hail—
    And then the hell began.

Broadside for broadside quick
   Set up a murderous roar;
Like thunder it resounded
   From echoing shore to shore.
This dreadful duel lasted
   Near a quarter-of-an-hour;
Then the *Chesapeake* drove right aboard,
   And put her in our power.

Our captain went to their ship's side
   To see how she did lie,
When he beheld the enemy's men,
   Who from their guns did fly.
'All hands for boarding!' now he cried.
   'The victory is sure!
Come, bear a hand, my gallant boys—
   Our prize we'll now secure!'

Like lions then we rushed aboard,
   And fought them hand to hand;
And tho' they did outnumber us,
   They could not us withstand.
They fought in desperation,
   Disorder and dismay,
And in about three minutes' time
   Were forced to give us way.

Their captain and lieutenant,
　　With seventy of the crew,
Were killed in this sharp action,
　　And a hundred wounded too;
The ship we took to Halifax,
　　And the captain buried there,
And the living of his crew
　　As his chief mourners were.

Have courage, all brave British tars,
　　And never be dismayed;
But put the can of grog about,
　　And drink success to trade;
Likewise to gallant Captain Broke
　　And all his valiant crew,
Who beat the bold Americans
　　And brought their courage to.

The Old Navy

Captain Charles Marryat

The captain stood on the carronade: 'First lieutenant,' says he
'Send all my merry men aft here, for they must list to me;
I haven't the gift of the gab, my sons—because I'm bred to
　　the sea;
That ship there is a Frenchman, who means to fight with *we*.
　　And *odds bobs, hammer and tongs*, long as I've been to sea,
　　I've fought 'gainst every odds—but I've gained the
　　　victory!

'That ship there is a Frenchman, and if we don't take she,
'Tis a thousand bullets to one, that she will capture we;
I haven't the gift of the gab, my boys; so each man to his
　　gun;
If she's not mine in half an hour, I'll flog each mother's son.
　　For *odds bobs, hammer and tongs*, long as I've been to sea,
　　I've fought 'gainst every odds—and I've gained the
　　　victory!'

We fought for twenty minutes, when the Frenchman had
    enough;
'I little thought,' said he, 'that your men were of such stuff;'
Our captain took the Frenchman's sword, a low bow made
    to he;
'I haven't the gift of the gab, monsieur, but polite I wish to
    be.
   And *odds bobs, hammer and tongs*, long as I've been to sea,
   I've fought 'gainst every odds—and I've gained the
       victory!'

Our captain sent for all of us: 'My merry men,' said he,
'I haven't the gift of the gab, my lads, but yet I thankful be:
You've done your duty handsomely, each man stood to his
    gun;
If you hadn't, you villains, as sure as day, I'd have flogged
    each mother's son,
   For *odds bobs, hammer and tongs*, as long as I'm at sea,
   I'll fight 'gainst every odds—and I'll gain the victory!'

Men who march away

Thomas Hardy

   We be the King's men, hale and hearty,
   Marching to meet one Buonaparty;
   If he won't sail, lest the wind should blow,
   We shall have marched for nothing, O!
           Right fol-lol!

We be the King's men, hale and hearty,
Marching to meet one Buonaparty;
If he be sea-sick, says 'No, no!'
We shall have marched for nothing, O!
                    Right fol-lol!

We be the King's men, hale and hearty,
Marching to meet one Buonaparty;
Never mind, mates; we'll be merry, though
We may have marched for nothing, O!
                    Right fol-lol!

Tom Bowling

Charles Dibdin

Here, a sheer hulk, lies poor Tom Bowling,
    The darling of our crew;
No more he'll hear the tempest howling,
    For Death has broached him to.
His form was of the manliest beauty,
    His heart was kind and soft;
Faithful below, he did his duty,
    But now he's gone aloft.

Tom never from his word departed,
    His virtues were so rare;
His friends were many and true-hearted,
    His Poll was kind and fair.
And then he'd sing so blithe and jolly;
    Ah, many's the time and oft!
But mirth is turned to melancholy,
    For Tom is gone aloft.

Yet shall poor Tom find pleasant weather,
   When He, who all commands,
Shall give, to call Life's crew together,
   The word to pipe all hands.
Thus Death, who Kings and Tars despatches,
   In vain Tom's life has doffed.
For though his body's under hatches,
   His soul is gone aloft.

The Burial of Sir John Moore
at Corunna, 1809
Charles Wolfe

Not a drum was heard, not a funeral note,
   As his corpse to the rampart we hurried;
Not a soldier discharged his farewell shot,
   O'er the grave where our hero we buried.

We buried him darkly, at dead of night,
   The sods with our bayonets turning;
By the struggling moonbeam's misty light,
   And the lantern dimly burning.

No useless coffin enclosed his breast,
   Not in sheet nor in shroud we wound him;
But he lay like a warrior taking his rest,
   With his martial cloak around him.

Few and short were the prayers we said,
   And we spoke not a word of sorrow;
But we steadfastly gazed on the face that was dead,
   And we bitterly thought of the morrow.

We thought, as we hollowed his narrow bed,
   And smoothed down his lonely pillow,
That the foe and the stranger would tread o'er his
     head,
   And we far away on the billow!

Lightly they'll talk of the spirit that's gone,
   And o'er his cold ashes upbraid him;
But little he'll reck, if they let him sleep on,
   In the grave where a Briton has laid him.

But half of our heavy task was done
   When the clock struck the hour for retiring;
And we heard the distant and random gun
   That the foe was sullenly firing.

Slowly and sadly we laid him down,
   From the field of his fame fresh and gory;
We carved not a line, and we raised not a stone—
   But we left him alone with his glory.

Soldier, Rest! Thy Warfare o'er

Sir Walter Scott

Soldier, rest! thy warfare o'er,
   Sleep the sleep that knows not breaking;
Dream of battled fields no more,
   Days of danger, nights of waking.
In our isle's enchanted hall,
   Hands unseen thy couch are strewing,
Fairy strains of music fall,
   Every sense in slumber dewing.
Soldier, rest! thy warfare o'er,
Dream of fighting-fields no more:
Sleep the sleep that knows not breaking,
Morn of toil, nor night of waking.

No rude sound shall reach thine ear,
    Armour's clang, or war-steed champing,
Trump nor pibroch summon here
    Mustering clan, or squadron tramping.
Yet the lark's shrill fife may come
    At the daybreak from the fallow,
And the bittern sound his drum,
    Booming from the sedgy shallow.
Ruder sounds shall none be near,
Guards nor warders challenge here,
Here's no war-steed's neigh and champing,
Shouting clans, or squadrons stamping.

The Question

Percy Bysshe Shelley

I dreamed that, as I wandered by the way,
    Bare winter suddenly was changed to spring,
And gentle odours led my steps astray,
    Mixed with a sound of waters murmuring
Along a shelving bank of turf, which lay
    Under a copse, and hardly dared to fling
Its green arms round the bosom of the stream,
But kissed it and then fled, as thou mightest in dream

There grew pied wind-flowers and violets,
    Daisies, those pearled Arcturi of the earth,
The constellated flower that never sets;
    Faint oxlips; tender bluebells, at whose birth
The sod scarce heaved; and that tall flower that wet
    Like a child, half in tenderness and mirth—
Its mother's face with heaven-collected tears,
When the low wind, its playmate's voice, it hear

And in the warm hedge grew lush eglantine,
  Green cowbind and the moonlight-coloured May,
And cherry blossoms, and white cups, whose wine
  Was the bright dew yet drained not by the day;
And wild roses, and ivy serpentine,
  With its dark buds and leaves, wandering astray;
And flowers azure, black and streaked with gold,
Fairer than any wakened eyes behold.

And nearer to the river's trembling edge
  There grew broad flag flowers, purple prankt with
    white,
And starry river buds among the sedge,
  And floating water-lilies, broad and bright,
Which lit the oak that overhung the hedge
  With moonlight beams of their own watery light;
And bulrushes, and reeds of such deep green
As soothed the dazzled eye with sober sheen.

Methought that of these visionary flowers
  I made a nosegay, bound in such a way
That the same hues, which in their natural bowers
  Were mingled or opposed, the like array
Kept these imprisoned children of the Hours
  Within my hand—and then, elate and gay,
I hastened to the spot whence I had come,
That I might there present it!—Oh, to whom?

A Nosegay
Edmund Spenser

Bring hether the Pincke and purple Cullambine,
    With Gelliflowres:
Bring Coronations, and Sops in wine,
    Worne of Paramoures.
Strowe me the ground with Daffadowndillies,
And Cowslips, and Kingcups, and loved Lillies:
    The pretie Pawnce,
    And the Chevisaunce,
Shall match with the fayre flowre Delice. . . .

Spring
Lord Tennyson

Now fades the last long streak of snow,
    Now burgeons every maze of quick
    About the flowering squares, and thick
By ashen roots the violets blow.

Now rings the woodland loud and long,
    The distance takes a lovelier hue,
    And drowned in yonder living blue
The lark becomes a sightless song.

Now dance the lights on lawn and lea,
    The flocks are whiter down the vale,
    And milkier every milky sail
On winding stream or distant sea;

Where now the seamew pipes, or dives
    In yonder greening gleam, and fly
    The happy birds, that change their sky
To build and brood, that live their lives

143

From land to land; and in my breast
  Spring wakens too; and my regret
  Becomes an April violet,
And buds and blossoms like the rest.

The Rooks

Percy Bysshe Shelley

'Mid the mountains Euganean
I stood listening to the pæan,
With which the legioned rooks did hail
The sun's uprise majestical;
Gathering round with wings all hoar,
Through the dewy mist they soar
Like grey shades, till the eastern heaven
Bursts, and then, as clouds of even,
Flecked with fire and azure, lie
In the unfathomable sky,
So their plumes of purple grain,
Starred with drops of golden rain,
Gleam above the sunlight woods,
As in silent multitudes
On the morning's fitful gale
Through the broken mist they sail,
And the vapours cloven and gleaming
Follow down the dark steep streaming,
Till all is bright, and clear, and still,
Round the solitary hill. . . .

Weathers

Thomas Hardy

This is the weather the cuckoo likes,
    And so do I;
When showers betumble the chestnut spikes,
    And nestlings fly;
And the little brown nightingale bills his best,
And they sit outside at 'The Travellers' Rest,'
And maids come forth sprig-muslin drest,
And citizens dream of the south and west,
    And so do I.

This is the weather the shepherd shuns,
    And so do I;
When beeches drip in browns and duns,
    And thresh, and ply;
The hill-hid tides throb, throe on throe,
And meadow rivulets overflow,
And drops on gate-bars hang in a row,
And rooks in families homeward go,
    And so do I.

The Brook

Lord Tennyson

I come from haunts of coot and hern,
    I make a sudden sally,
And sparkle out among the fern,
    To bicker down a valley.

By thirty hills I hurry down,
    Or slip between the ridges,
By twenty thorps, a little town,
    And half a hundred bridges.

Till last by Philip's farm I flow,
  To join the brimming river,
For men may come and men may go,
  But I go on for ever.

I chatter over stony ways,
  In little sharps and trebles,
I bubble into eddying bays,
  I babble on the pebbles.

With many a curve my banks I fret
  By many a field and fallow,
And many a fairy foreland set
  With willow-weed and mallow.

I chatter, chatter, as I flow
  To join the brimming river,
For men may come and men may go,
  But I go on for ever.

I wind about, and in and out,
  With here a blossom sailing,
And here and there a lusty trout,
  And here and there a grayling.

And here and there a foamy flake
  Upon me, as I travel
With many a silvery waterbreak
  Above the golden gravel,

And draw them all along, and flow
  To join the brimming river,
For men may come and men may go,
  But I go on for ever.

I steal by lawns and grassy plots,
    I slide by hazel covers;
I move the sweet forget-me-nots
    That grow for happy lovers.

I slip, I slide, I gloom, I glance,
    Among my skimming swallows;
I make the netted sunbeam dance
    Against my sandy shallows.

I murmur under moon and stars
    In brambly wildernesses;
I linger by my shingly bars;
    I loiter round my cresses;

And out again I curve and flow
    To join the brimming river,
For men may come and men may go,
    But I go on for ever.

Under the Greenwood Tree

William Shakespeare

Under the greenwood tree
Who loves to lie with me,
And tune his merry note
Unto the sweet bird's throat,
Come hither, come hither, come hither;
    Here shall he see
    No enemy
But winter and rough weather.

Who doth ambition shun,
And loves to live in the sun,
Seeking the food he eats,
And pleased with what he gets,
Come hither, come hither, come hither:
Here shall he see
No enemy
But winter and rough weather.

Elves' Song
Ben Jonson

Buz! quoth the blue fly;
Hum! quoth the bee:
Buz! and Hum! they cry,
And so do we.
In his ear, in his nose,
Thus do you see?
He ate the dormouse:
Else it was he.

Song
Samuel Taylor Coleridge

A sunny shaft did I behold,
From sky to earth it slanted,
And poised therein a bird so bold,
Sweet bird, thou wert enchanted!
He sank, he rose, he twinkled, he trolled
Within that shaft of sunny mist;
His eyes of fire, his beak of gold,
All else of amethyst.

And thus he sang, 'Adieu! adieu!
Lòve's drèams prove seldom true.
The blossoms they make no delay,
The sparkling dewdrops will not stay.
   Sweet month of May,
   We must away,
   Far, far away!
   To-day! to-day!'

A Drop of Dew

Andrew Marvell

See how the orient dew
Shed from the bosom of the morn
   Into the blowing roses,
Yet careless of its mansion new,
For the clear region where 'twas born,
   Round in itself encloses;
And in its little globe's extent
Frames as it can its native element.
   How it the purple flower does slight,
Scarce touching where it lies!
But, gazing back upon the skies,
   Shines with a mournful light. . . .

Shadows

Eleanor Farjeon

When Shadows from the East are long,
Then Larks go up for Morning-Song.
When Shadows are not seen at all,
Then Green-Leaves into Silence fall.
When Shadows from the West grow long,
Then Blackbirds meet for Evensong.

Midnight

Thomas Sackville, Lord Buckhurst

Midnight was come, and every vital thing
With sweet sound sleep their weary limbs did rest:
The beasts were still, the little birds that sing
Now sweetly slept besides their mothers' breast,
The old and all were shrouded in their nest.
The waters calm, the cruel seas did cease,
The woods, the fields, and all things held their peace.

The golden stars were whirled amid their race,
And on the earth did laugh with twinkling light,
When each thing, nestled in his resting place,
Forgot day's pain with pleasure of the night . . .

The Fruit Plucker

Samuel Taylor Coleridge

Encinctured with a twine of leaves,
That leafy twine his only dress,
A lovely Boy was plucking fruits,
By moonlight, in a wilderness,
The moon was bright, the air was free,
And fruits and flowers together grew
On many a shrub and many a tree:
And all put on a gentle hue,
Hanging in the shadowy air
Like a picture rich and rare.

It was a climate where, they say,
The night is more beloved than day.
But who that beauteous Boy beguiled,
That beauteous Boy to linger here?
Alone, by night, a little child,
In place so silent and so wild—
Has he no friend, no loving mother near?

The Sick Child

Robert Louis Stevenson

'O mother, lay your hand on my brow!
O mother, mother, where am I now?
Why is the room so gaunt and great?
Why am I lying awake so late?'

'Fear not at all: the night is still.
Nothing is here that means you ill—
Nothing but lamps the whole town through,
And never a child awake but you.'

'Mother, mother, speak low in my ear,
Some of the things are so great and near,
Some are so small and far away,
I have a fear that I cannot say.
What have I done, and what do I fear,
And why are you crying, mother dear?'

'Out in the city, sounds begin.
Thank the kind God, the carts come in!
An hour or two more, and God is so kind,
The day shall be blue in the window-blind,
Then shall my child go sweetly asleep,
To dream of the birds and the hills of sheep.'

The Nightingale
Samuel Taylor Coleridge

        . . . I know a grove
Of large extent, hard by a castle huge,
Which the great lord inhabits not; and so
This grove is wild with tangling underwood,
And the trim walks are broken up, and grass,
Thin grass and king-cups grow within the paths.
But never elsewhere in one place I knew
So many nightingales; and far and near,
In wood and thicket, over the wide grove,
They answer and provoke each other's song,
With skirmish and capricious passagings,
And murmurs musical and swift *jug-jug*,
And one low piping sound more sweet than all—
Stirring the air with such a harmony,
That should you close your eyes, you might almost
Forget it was not day! On moonlit bushes,
Whose dewy leaflets are but half disclosed,
You may perchance behold them on the twigs,
Their bright, bright eyes, their eyes both bright and full,
Glistening, while many a glow-worm in the shade
Lights up her love-torch . . .

Thy Sweet Voice
From *Stanzas for Music*
Lord Byron

    There be none of beauty's daughters
        With a magic like thee;
    And like music on the waters
        Is thy sweet voice to me:
    When, as if its sound were causing
    The charmed ocean's pausing,
    The waves lie still and gleaming,
    And the lulled winds seem dreaming. . . .

A Comparison

Ben Jonson

Have you seen but a bright lily grow,
  Before rude hands have touched it?
Have you marked but the fall of the snow
  Before the soil hath smutched it?
    Have you felt the wool of the beaver,
    Or swan's down ever?
  Or have smelt o' the bud o' the briar,
  Or the nard i' the fire?
Or have tasted the bag o' the bee?
O so whìte, O so sòft, O so swèet is *she*.

The Light of Other Days

Thomas Moore

Oft in the stilly night
  Ere slumber's chain has bound me,
Fond Memory brings the light
  Of other days around me:
    The smiles, the tears
    Of boyhood's years,
  The words of love then spoken;
    The eyes that shone,
    Now dimmed and gone,
  The cheerful hearts now broken!
Thus in the stilly night
  Ere slumber's chain has bound me,
Sad Memory brings the light
  Of other days around me.

When I remember all
  The friends so linked together
I've seen around me fall
  Like leaves in wintry weather,

I feel like one
Who treads alone
Some banquet-hall deserted,
Whose lights are fled,
Whose garlands dead,
And all but he departed!
Thus in the stilly night
Ere slumber's chain has bound me,
Sad Memory brings the light
Of other days around me.

Absence

When I think on the happy days
I spent wi' you, my dearie;
And now what lands between us lie,
How can I be but eerie!

How slow ye move, ye heavy hours,
As ye were wae and weary!
It wasna sae ye glinted by
When I was wi' my dearie.

Robin Adair

Caroline Keppel

What's this dull town to me?
Robin's not near;
What was't I wished to see,
What wished to hear?
Where's all the joy and mirth
That made this town a heaven on earth?
Oh! they're all fled with thee,
Robin Adair.

What made the assembly shine?
   Robin Adair;
What made the ball so fine?
   Robin was there.
What, when the day was o'er,
What made my heart so sore?
Oh! it was parting with
   Robin Adair.

But now thou'rt far from me,
   Robin Adair;
And now I never see
   Robin Adair;
Yet he I love so well,
Still in my heart shall dwell,
Oh! I can ne'er forget
   Robin Adair.

A Widow Bird

Percy Bysshe Shelley

A widow bird sate mourning for her love
   Upon a wintry bough;
The frozen wind crept on above,
   The freezing stream below.

There was no leaf upon the forest bare,
   No flower upon the ground,
And little motion in the air
   Except the mill-wheel's sound.

Song

R. M. Milnes

I wandered by the brook-side,
  I wandered by the mill,
I could not hear the brook flow,
  The noisy wheel was still;
There was no burr of grasshopper,
  No chirp of any bird;
But the beating of my own heart
  Was all the sound I heard.

I sat beneath the elm-tree,
  I watched the long, long shade,
And as it grew still longer
  I did not feel afraid;
For I listened for a footfall,
  I listened for a word—
But the beating of my own heart
  Was all the sound I heard.

He came not—no, he came not;
  The night came on alone;
The little stars sat one by one
  Each on his golden throne;
The evening air passed by my cheek,
  The leaves above were stirred—
But the beating of my own heart
  Was all the sound I heard.

Fast silent tears were flowing,
  When some one stood behind;
A hand was on my shoulder,
  I knew its touch was kind;
It drew me nearer—nearer;
  We did not speak a word—
For the beating of our own hearts
  Was all the sound we heard.

Vailima

Blows the wind to-day, and the sun and the rain are flying,
   Blows the wind on the moors to-day and now,
Where about the graves of the martyrs the whaups are
      crying,
   My heart remembers how!

Grey recumbent tombs of the dead in desert places,
   Standing stones on the vacant wine-red moor,
Hills of sheep, and the howes of the silent vanished races,
   And winds, austere and pure:

Be it granted me to behold you again in dying,
   Hills of home! and to hear again the call;
Hear about the graves of the martyrs the peewees crying,
   And hear no more at all.

The Deserted House

Mary Coleridge

There's no smoke in the chimney,
   And the rain beats on the floor;
There's no glass in the window,
   There's no wood in the door;
The heather grows behind the house,
   And the sand lies before.

No hand hath trained the ivy,
   The walls are gray and bare;
The boats upon the sea sail by,
   Nor ever tarry there.
No beast of the field comes nigh,
   Nor any bird of the air.

157

The Trees are bare

From *The Bluebell*

Emily Brontë

The trees are bare, the sun is cold,
   And seldom, seldom seen;
The heavens have lost their zone of gold,
   And earth her robe of green;

And ice upon the glancing stream
   Has cast its sombre shade;
The distant hills and valleys seem
   In frozen mist arrayed. . . .

And, oh! when chill the sunbeams fall
   Adown that dreary sky,
And gild yon dank and darkened wall
   With transient brilliancy,

How do I weep, how do I pine
   For the time of flowers to come,
And turn me from that fading shrine,
   To mourn the fields of home!

I had a Dove

John Keats

I had a dove and the sweet dove died;
   And I have thought it died of grieving:
O, what could it grieve for? Its feet were tied
   With a silken thread of my own hand's weaving;
   Sweet little red feet! why should you die—
Why should you leave me, sweet bird! Why?
You lived alone in the forest-tree,
Why, pretty thing! would you not live with me?
I kissed you oft and gave you white peas;
Why not live sweetly, as in the green trees?

Ophelia's Song

William Shakespeare

How should I your true love know
  From another one?
By his cockle hat and staff,
  And his sandal shoon.

He is dead and gone, lady,
  He is dead and gone;
At his head a grass-green turf;
  At his heels a stone.

White his shroud as the mountain snow,
  Larded with sweet flowers;
Which bewept to the grave did go
  With true-love showers.

The Shower

Beatrice Eve

Beneath the green Acacia tree
  The scarlet barrel organ stands,
Its painted cherubs clasping wreaths
  Of dusty roses in their hands.

The young dark-eyed Italian boy
  Who grinds the tune with weary ease
Raises his head to scan the clouds
  That gather dark above the trees.

The organ plays a plaintive song
  Of one who wore a purple gown;
Swift through the green Acacia tree
  The silver rain comes falling down.

Yet still the painted cherubs smile
    With tears upon their painted eyes;
The dark-eyed boy with drooping head
    Leans on the organ-box and sighs.

.   .   .   .   .

The rainbow spreads her coloured veil;
    The shower is past; the air is sweet;
With happy cries the children come,
    Skipping and tumbling down the street.

With graceful steps they dance between
    The silver-shining pools of rain;
The organ plays a jingling tune;
    The dark boy nods and smiles again.

The Rain

W. H. Davies

I hear leaves drinking Rain;
    I hear rich leaves on top
Giving the poor beneath
    Drop after drop;
'Tis a sweet noise to hear
These green leaves drinking near.

And when the Sun comes out,
    After this Rain shall stop,
A wondrous Light will fill
    Each dark, round drop;
I hope the Sun shines bright:
'Twill be a lovely sight.

The Storm

Edward Shanks

We wake to hear the storm come down,
    Sudden on roof and pane;
The thunder's loud and the hasty wind
    Hurries the beating rain.

The rain slackens, the wind blows gently,
    The gust grows gentle and stills,
And the thunder, like a breaking stick,
    Stumbles about the hills.

The drops still hang on leaf and thorn,
    The downs stand up more green;
The sun comes out again in power
    And the sky is washed and clean.

The Poplar Field

William Cowper

The poplars are felled, farewell to the shade,
And the whispering sound of the cool colonnade;
The winds play no longer and sing in the leaves,
Nor Ouse on his bosom their image receives.

Twelve years have elapsed, since I last took a view
Of my favourite field, and the bank where they grew;
And now in the grass behold they are laid,
And the tree is my seat, that once lent me a shade.

The blackbird has fled to another retreat,
Where the hazels afford him a screen from the heat;
And the scene, where his melody charmed me before,
Resounds with his sweet-flowing ditty no more. . . .

One Lime

Eleanor Farjeon

One lime in Alfriston made sweet,
   So sweet, the August night,
That all the air along the street,
The shadowed air in the shadowed street,
   Was swimming in delight.

If any bee had lingered there
   She might have spent her time
In filling combs from that fragrant air,
Her golden combs from the golden air,
   And never seen the lime.

The Whirl-Blast

William Wordsworth

A whirl-blast from behind the hill
Rushed o'er the woods with startling sound;
Then—all at once the air was still,
And showers of hailstones pattered round.
Where leafless oaks towered high above,
I sat within an undergrove
Of tallest hollies, tall and green;
A fairer bower was never seen.
From year to year the spacious floor
With withered leaves is covered o'er,
And all the year the bower is green;
But see! where'er the hailstones drop
The withered leaves all skip and hop;
There's not a breeze—no breath of air—
Yet here, and there, and everywhere
Along the floor, beneath the shade
By those embowering hollies made,

The leaves in myriads jump and spring,
As if with pipes and music rare
Some Robin Goodfellow were there,
And all those leaves, in festive glee,
Were dancing to the minstrelsy.

Windy Nights

Robert Louis Stevenson

Whenever the moon and stars are set,
  Whenever the wind is high,
All night long in the dark and wet,
  A man goes riding by.
Late in the night when the fires are out,
Why does he gallop and gallop about?

Whenever the trees are crying aloud,
  And ships are tossed at sea,
By, on the highway, low and loud,
  By at the gallop goes he;
By at the gallop he goes, and then
By he comes back at the gallop again.

To Autumn

John Keats

Season of mists and mellow fruitfulness,
  Close bosom-friend of the maturing sun;
Conspiring with him how to load and bless
  With fruit the vines that round the thatch-eaves run;
To bend with apples the mossed cottage-trees,
  And fill all fruit with ripeness to the core;
    To swell the gourd, and plump the hazel shells
  With a sweet kernel; to set budding more,
And still more, later flowers for the bees,
Until they think warm days will never cease,
    For Summer has o'er-brimmed their clammy cells.

Who hath not seen thee oft amid thy store?
  Sometimes whoever seeks abroad may find
Thee sitting careless on a granary floor,
  Thy hair soft-lifted by the winnowing wind;
Or on a half-reaped furrow sound asleep,
  Drowsed with the fume of poppies, while thy hook
    Spares the next swath and all its twinèd flowers:
And sometimes like a gleaner thou dost keep
  Steady thy laden head across a brook;
  Or by a cider-press, with patient look,
    Thou watchest the last oozings hours by hours.

Where are the songs of Spring? Ay, where are they?
  Think not of them, thou hast thy music too—
While barrèd clouds bloom the soft-dying day,
  And touch the stubble-plains with rosy hue;
Then in a wailful choir the small gnats mourn
  Among the river sallows, borne aloft
    Or sinking as the light wind lives or dies;
And full-grown lambs loud bleat from hilly bourn;
  Hedge-crickets sing; and now with treble soft
  The red-breast whistles from a garden-croft;
    And gathering swallows twitter in the skies.

The Equinox

H. W. Longfellow

When descends on the Atlantic
The gigantic
  Storm-wind of the equinox,
Landward in his wrath he scourges
The toiling surges,
  Laden with seaweed from the rocks.

From Bermuda's reefs; from the edges
Of sunken ledges
   In some far-off, bright Azore;
From Bahama, and the dashing,
Silver-flashing
   Surges of San Salvador;

From the tumbling surf, that buries
The Orkneyan skerries,
   Answering the hoarse Hebrides;
And from wrecks of ships, and drifting
Spars, uplifting
   On the desolate, rainy seas:

Ever drifting, drifting, drifting
On the shifting
   Currents of the restless main;
Till in sheltered coves and reaches
Of sandy beaches
   All have found repose again.

The Windmill

E. V. Lucas

If you should bid me make a choice
   'Twixt wind and water mill,
In spite of all the millpond's charms
I'd take those gleaming sweeping arms
   High on a windy hill.

The miller stands before his door
   And whistles for a breeze;
And, when it comes, his sails go round
With such a mighty rushing sound
   You think of heavy seas.

And if the wind declines to blow
    The miller takes a nap
(Although he'd better spend an hour
In brushing at the dust and flour
    That line his coat and cap).

Now, if a water-mill were his,
    Such rest he'd never know,
For round and round his crashing wheel,
His dashing, splashing, plashing wheel,
    Unceasingly would go.

So, if you'd bid me make a choice
    'Twixt wind and water mill,
In spite of all a millpond's charms,
I'd take those gleaming sweeping arms
    High on the windy hill.

Who has seen the Wind?

Christina Rossetti

Who has seen the wind?
    Neither I nor you:
But when the leaves hang trembling,
    The wind is passing through.

Who has seen the wind?
    Neither you nor I:
But when the trees bow down their heads,
    The wind is passing by.

Winter
James Thomson

Through the hushed air the whitening shower descends,
At first thin wavering; till at last the flakes
Fall broad, and wide, and fast, dimming the day,
With a continual flow. The cherished fields
Put on their winter-robe of purest white.
'Tis brightness all; save where the new snow melts
Along the mazy current. Low the woods
Bow their hoar head; and ere the languid sun
Faint from the west emits his evening ray,
Earth's universal face, deep hid, and chill,
Is one wild dazzling waste, that buries wide
The works of man. Drooping, the labourer-ox
Stands covered o'er with snow, and then demands
The fruit of all his toil. The fowls of Heaven,
Tamed by the cruel season, crowd around
The winnowing store, and claim the little boon
Which Providence assigns them. One alone,
The redbreast, sacred to the household gods,
Wisely regardful of the embroiling sky,
In joyless fields and thorny thickets, leaves
His shivering mates, and pays to trusted man
His annual visit. Half afraid, he first
Against the window beats; then, brisk, alights
On the warm hearth; then, hopping o'er the floor,
Eyes all the smiling family askance,
And pecks, and starts, and wonders where he is;
Till more familiar grown, the table-crumbs
Attract his slender feet. The foodless wilds
Pour forth their brown inhabitants. The hare,
Though timorous of heart, and hard beset
By death in various forms, dark snares and dogs,
And more unpitying men, the garden seeks,
Urged on by fearless want. . . .

Blow, blow

William Shakespeare

Blow, blow, thou winter wind,
Thou art not so unkind
    As man's ingratitude;
Thy tooth is not so keen,
Because thou art not seen,
    Although thy breath be rude.
Heigh-ho! sing, *heigh-ho!* unto the green holly:
Most friendship is feigning, most loving mere folly.
    Then heigh-ho! the holly!
    This life is most jolly.

Freeze, freeze, thou bitter sky,
That dost not bite so nigh
    As benefits forgot:
Though thou the waters warp,
Thy sting is not so sharp
    As friend remembered not.
Heigh-ho! sing, *heigh-ho!* unto the green holly:
Most friendship is feigning, most loving mere folly.
    Then *heigh-ho!* the holly!
    This life is most jolly.

A Thanksgiving to God
for His House

Robert Herrick

Lord, Thou hast given me a cell
    Wherein to dwell;
A little house, whose humble Roof
    Is weather-proof;
Under the spars of which I lie
    Both soft, and dry;

Where Thou my chamber for to ward
    Hast set a Guard
Of harmless thoughts, to watch and keep
    Me, while I sleep.
Low is my porch, as is my Fate,
    Both void of state;
And yet the threshold of my door
    Is worn by the poor,
Who thither come, and freely get
    Good words, or meat:
Like as my Parlour, so my Hall
    And Kitchen's small:
A little Buttery, and therein
    A little Bin,
Which keeps my little loaf of Bread
    Unchipped, unfled:
Some brittle sticks of Thorn or Briar
    Make me a fire,
Close by whose living coal I sit,
    And glow like it.
Lord, I confess too, when I dine,
    The pulse is Thine,
And all those other Bits, that be
    There placed by Thee;
The Worts, the Purslane, and the Mess
    Of Water-cress,
Which of Thy kindness Thou hast sent;
    And my content
Makes those, and my beloved Beet,
    To be more sweet.
'Tis Thou that crown'st my glittering Hearth
    With guiltless mirth;
And giv'st me Wassail Bowls to drink,
  Spiced to the brink.
Lord, 'tis thy plenty-dropping hand
    That soils my land;

And giv'st me, for my Bushel sown,
  Twice ten for one:
Thou mak'st my teeming Hen to lay
  Her egg each day:
Besides my healthful Ewes to bear
  Me twins each year:
The while the conduits of my Kine
  Run Cream, (for Wine).
All these, and better, Thou dost send
  Me, to this end,
That I should render, for my part,
  A thankful heart;
Which, fired with incense, I resign,
  As wholly Thine;
But the acceptance, that must be,
  My Christ, by Thee.

The Year's Round

Coventry Patmore

The crocus, while the days are dark,
  Unfolds its saffron sheen;
At April's touch, the crudest bark
  Discovers gems of green.

Then sleep the seasons, full of might;
  While slowly swells the pod
And rounds the peach, and in the night
  The mushroom bursts the sod.

The Winter falls; the frozen rut
  Is bound with silver bars;
The snow-drift heaps against the hut,
  And night is pierced with stars.

170

The Wife of Usher's Well

There lived a wife at Usher's Well,
    And a wealthy wife was she;
She had three stout and stalwart sons,
    And sent them o'er the sea.

They hadna been a week from her,
    A week but barely ane,
When word came to the carline wife
    That her three sons were gane.

They hadna been a week from her,
    A week but barely three,
When word came to the carline wife
    That her sons she'd never see.

'I wish the wind may never cease,
    Nor fashes in the flood,
Till my three sons come hame to me
    In earthly flesh and blood!'

It fell about the Martinmas,
    When nights are lang and mirk,
The carline wife's three sons came hame,
    And their hats were o' the birk.

It neither grew in syke nor ditch,
    Nor yet in ony sheugh;
But at the gates o' Paradise
    That birk grew fair eneugh.

'Blow up the fire, my maidens!
    Bring water from the well!
For a' my house shall feast this night,
    Since my three sons are well.'

And she has made to them a bed,
    She's made it large and wide;
And she's ta'en her mantle her about,
    Sat down at the bedside.

Up then crew the red, red cock,
    And up and crew the gray;
The eldest to the youngest said,
    ''Tis time we were away.'

The cock he hadna craw'd but once,
    And clapp'd his wings at a',
When the youngest to the eldest said,
    'Brother, we must awa'.

'The cock doth craw, the day doth daw,
    The channerin' worm doth chide;
Gin we be miss'd out of our place,
    A sair pain we maun bide.'

'Lie still, lie still but a little wee while,
    Lie still but if we may;
Gin my mother should miss us when she wakes,
    She'll go mad ere it be day.'

'Fare ye weel, my mother dear!
    Fareweel to barn and byre!
And fare ye weel, the bonny lass
    That kindles my mother's fire!'

The Dream

There was a lady fair and gay,
    And children she had three:
She sent them away to some northern land,
    For to learn their grammeree.

They hadn't been gone but a very short time,
    About three months to a day,
When sickness came to that far land
    And swept those babes away. . . .

It was about one Christmas time,
    When the nights were long and cool,
She dreamed of her three little lonely babes
    Come running in their mother's room.

The table was fixed and the cloth was spread,
    And on it put bread and wine:
'Come sit you down, my three little babes,
    And eat and drink of mine.'

'We will neither eat your bread, dear mother,
    Nor we'll neither drink your wine;
For to our Saviour we must return
    To-night or in the morning syne.'

The bed was fixed in the back room;
    On it was some clean white sheet,
And on the top was a golden cloth,
    To make those little babies sleep.

'Wake up! wake up!' says the oldest one,
    'Wake up! it's almost day.
And to our Saviour we must return
    This night, for we are long away.'

'Green grass grows at our head, dear mother,
    Green moss grows at our feet;
The tears that you shed for us three babes
    Won't wet our winding sheet.'

As Joseph was awakening

As Joseph was a-waukin',
  He heard an angel sing,
'This night shall be the birthnight
  Of Christ our heavenly King.

'His birth-bed shall be neither
  In housen nor in hall,
Nor in the place of paradise,
  But in the oxen's stall.

'He neither shall be rockèd
  In silver nor in gold,
But in the wooden manger
  That lieth in the mould.

'He neither shall be washen
  With white wine nor with red,
But with the fair spring water
  That on you shall be shed.

'He neither shall be clothèd
  In purple nor in pall,
But in the fair, white linen
  That usen babies all.'

As Joseph was a-waukin',
  Thus did the angel sing,
And Mary's son at midnight
  Was born to be our King.

Then be you glad, good people,
  At this time of the year;
And light you up your candles,
  For His star it shineth clear.

I sing of a Maiden

I sing of a maiden
   That is makeless;
King of all kings
   To her son she ches.

He came all so still
   Where his mother was,
As dew in April
   That falleth on the grass.

He came all so still
   To his mother's bower,
As dew in April
   That falleth on the flower.

He came all so still
   Where his mother lay,
As dew in April
   That falleth on the spray.

Mother and maiden
   Was never none but she;
Well may such a lady
   Godes mother be.

Children's Song of the Nativity

Frances Chesterton

How far is it to Bethlehem?
    Not very far.
Shall we find the stable-room
    Lit by a star?

Can we see the little child,
    Is he within?
If we lift the wooden latch
    May we go in?

May we stroke the creatures there,
    Ox, ass, or sheep?
May we peep like them and see
    Jesus asleep?

If we touch his tiny hand
    Will he awake?
Will he know we've come so far
    Just for his sake?

Great kings have precious gifts,
    And we have naught,
Little smiles and little tears
    Are all we brought.

For all weary children
    Mary must weep.
Here, on his bed of straw
    Sleep, children, sleep.

God in his mother's arms,
    Babes in the byre,
Sleep, as they sleep who find
    Their heart's desire.

Lambs

Katharine Tynan

I saw the ewes lying,
Their lambs bleating and crying,
Poor lambs, weary of travel, on the green sod.
Sore-foot, crying and bleating,
Each sweet to its sweeting—
And thought of another lamb, the Lamb of God.

In the sweet May so tender,
With trees in their new splendour,
I heard a lamb cry for its milky dam,
With a low bleat and weary,
As one dear to its dearie—
And thought on another lamb, dear Mary's lamb.

Each lamb beside its mother,
Its own, not any other,
Comforted with her milk, lay sweetly at rest,
Full fed and safe from harm,
As a child in the mother's arm—
I thought of a downy head at Mary's breast.

I saw the lambs playing,
No darling lost or straying,
About their mothers on the dewy heath,
Around the daisies and clover,
Each small love by its lover—
And thought of Mary's boy in Nazareth.

A lamb so soft and curled—
O sweetest name in the world!
The child, the Son, the Lamb; O heavenly Name!
That holds in its completeness
All lovely things and sweetness—
The Holy Spirit's thought for the Son—'God's
Lamb.'

The Pilgrim

John Bunyan

Who would true valour see,
  Let him come hither!
One here will constant be
  Come wind, come weather;
There's no discouragement
Shall make him once relent
His first-avowed intent
  To be a Pilgrim.

Whoso beset him round
  With dismal stories,
Do but themselves confound;
  His strength the more is.
No lion can him fright;
He'll with a giant fight;
But he will have a right
  To be a Pilgrim.

Hobgoblin, nor foul fiend,
  Can daunt his spirit;
He knows he at the end
  Shall Life inherit:-
Then, fancies, fly away;
Hè'll nòt fear what men say;
He'll labour, night and day,
  To be a Pilgrim.

To a Waterfowl

William Cullen Bryant

Whither, midst falling dew,
While glow the heavens with the last steps of day,
Far, through their rosy depths, dost thou pursue
    Thy solitary way?

Vainly the fowler's eye
Might mark thy distant flight to do thee wrong,
As, darkly seen against the crimson sky,
    Thy figure floats along.

Seek'st thou the plashy brink
Of weedy lake, or marge of river wide,
Or where the rocking billows rise and sink
    On the chafed ocean-side?

There is a Power whose care
Teaches thy way along that pathless coast—
The desert and illimitable air—
    Lone-wandering but not lost.

All day thy wings have fanned,
At that far height, the cold thin atmosphere,
Yet stoop not, weary, to the welcome land,
    Though the dark night is near.

And soon that toil shall end;
Soon shalt thou find a summer home, and rest
And scream among thy fellows; reeds shall bend
    Soon o'er thy sheltered nest.

Thou'rt gone—the abyss of heaven
Hath swallowed up thy form; yet on my heart
Deeply hath sunk the lesson thou hast given,
    And shall not soon depart.

He who, from zone to zone,
Guides through the boundless sky thy certain flight,
In the long way that I must tread alone,
Will lead my steps aright.

Epitaph on a Jacobite
Lord Macaulay

To my true king I offered free from stain
Courage and faith; vain faith, and courage vain.
For him I threw lands, honours, wealth away,
And one dear hope, that was more prized than they.
For him I languished in a foreign clime,
Gray-haired with sorrow in my manhood's prime;
Heard on Lavernia Scargill's whispering trees,
And pined by Arno for my lovelier Tees;
Beheld each night my home in fevered sleep,
Each morning started from the dream to weep;
Till God, who saw me tried too sorely, gave
The resting-place I asked, an early grave.
O thou, whom chance leads to this nameless stone,
From that proud country which was once mine own,
By those white cliffs I never more must see,
By that dear language which I spake like thee,
Forget all feuds, and shed one English tear
O'er English dust. A broken heart lies here.

Hame, Hame, Hame
Allan Cunningham

Hame, hame, hame, hame fain wad I be;
O hame, hame, hame to my ain countrie!

When the flower is in the bud, and the leaf is on the tree,
The lark shall sing me hame to my ain countrie.
Hame, hame, hame! O hame fain wad I be!
O hame, hame, hame to my ain countrie! . . .

King Charles

As I was going by Charing Cross,
I saw a black màn upon a black horse;
They told me it was King Charles the First;
Oh, dear! my heart was ready to burst!

The Spring is past
Chidiock Tichborne

The spring is past, and yet it hath not sprung;
    The fruit is dead, and yet the leaves are green;
My youth is gone, and yet I am but young;
    I saw the world, and yet I was not seen;
My thread is cut, and yet it is not spun;
And now I live, and now my life is done! . . .

That Wind
Emily Brontë

That wind, I used to hear it swelling
With joy divinely deep;
You might have seen my hot tears welling,
But rapture made me weep.

I used to love on winter nights
To lie, and dream alone
Of all the rare and real delights
My lonely years had known.

And oh! above the best of those
That coming time should bear,
Like heaven's own glorious stars they rose,
Still beaming bright and fair.

The Sands of Dee

Charles Kingsley

'O Mary, go and call the cattle home,
    And call the cattle home,
    And call the cattle home
  Across the sands of Dee';
The western wind was wild and dank with foam,
  And all alone went she.

The western tide crept up along the sand,
    And o'er and o'er the sand,
    And round and round the sand,
  As far as eye could see.
The rolling mist came down and hid the land:
  And never home came she.

'Oh! is it weed, or fish, or floating hair—
    A tress of golden hair,
    A drownèd maiden's hair
  Above the nets at sea?
Was never salmon yet that shone so fair
  Among the stakes on Dee.'

They rowed her in across the rolling foam,
    The cruel crawling foam,
    The cruel hungry foam,
  To her grave beside the sea:
But still the boatmen hear her call the cattle home
  Across the sands of Dee.

The Tide rises, the Tide falls

H. W. Longfellow

The tide rises, the tide falls,
The twilight darkens, the curlew calls;
Along the sea-sands damp and brown
The traveller hastens toward the town;
    And the tide rises, the tide falls.

Darkness settles on roofs and walls,
 But the sea in the darkness calls and calls;
The little waves, with their soft white hands,
Efface the footprints in the sands,
    And the tide rises, the tide falls.

The morning breaks; the steeds in their stalls
Stamp and neigh, as the hostler calls;
The day returns; but nevermore
Returns the traveller to the shore,
    And the tide rises, the tide falls.

A High Tide on the Coast of Lincolnshire

Jean Ingelow

The old mayor climbed the belfry tower,
  The ringers ran by two, by three;
'Pull, if ye never pulled before;
  Good ringers, pull your best,' quoth he.
'Play uppe, play uppe, O Boston bells!
Play all your changes, all your swells,
  Play uppe "The Brides of Enderby!"'

Men say it was a stolen tyde—
    The Lord that sent it, he knows all;
But in myne ears doth still abide
    The message that the bells let fall:
And there was naught of strange, beside
The flight of mews and peewits pied,
    By millions crouched on the old sea-wall.

I sat and spun within the doore,
    My thread brake off, I raised myne eyes!
The level sun, like ruddy ore,
    Lay sinking in the barren skies;
And dark against day's golden death
She moved where Lindis wandereth—
    My sonne's fair wife Elizabeth.

'Cusha! Cusha! Cusha!' calling,
Ere the early dews were falling,
    Farre away I heard her song.
    'Cusha! Cusha!' all along,
Where the reedy Lindis floweth,
Floweth, floweth,
From the meads where melick groweth
    Faintly came her milking song.

'Cusha! Cusha! Cusha!' calling,
'For the dews will soone be falling;
Leave your meadow grasses mellow,
Mellow, mellow;
Quit your cowslips, cowslips yellow;
    Còme uppe, Whitefoot, come uppe, Lightfoot,
Come uppe, Jetty, rise and follow,
    Jetty, to the milking-shed.'

If it be long, aye, long ago,
    When I beginne to think howe long,
Againe I hear the Lindis flow,
    Swift as an arrowe, sharpe and strong;
And all the aire it seemeth mee
Be full of floating bells (sayth shee),
That ring the tune of Enderby.

Alle fresh the level pasture lay,
    And not a shadow mote be seene,
Save where, full fyve good miles away,
    The steeple towered from out the greene;
And lo! the great bell farre and wide
Was heard in all the countryside
That Saturday at eventide.

The swanherds where their sedges are
    Moved on in sunset's golden breath,
The shepherde lads I heard afarre,
    And my sonne's wife, Elizabeth;
Till floating o'er the grassy sea
Came downe that kyndly message free,
'The Brides of Mavis Enderby.'

Then some looked uppe into the sky,
    And all along where Lindis flows
To where the goodly vessels lie,
    And where the lordly steeple shows,
They sayde, 'And why should this thing be,
What danger lowers by land or sea?
They ring the tune of Enderby!

'For evil news from Mablethorpe,
　　Of pyrate galleys warping downe;
For shippes ashore beyond the scorpe,
　　They have not spared to wake the towne;
But while the west bin red to see,
And storms be none, and pyrates flee,
Why ring "The Brides of Enderby"?'

I looked without, and lo! my sonne
　　Came riding downe with might and main.
He raised a shout as he drew on,
　　Till all the welkin rang again,
'Elizabeth! Elizabeth!'
(A sweeter woman ne'er drew breath
Than my sonne's wife, Elizabeth)

'The olde sea wall (he cried) is downe,
　　The rising tide comes on apace,
And boats adrift in yonder towne
　　Go sailing uppe the market-place.'
He shook as one that looks on death:
'God save you, mother!' straight he saith;
'Where is my wife, Elizabeth?'

'Good sonne, where Lindis winds away
　　With her two bairns I marked her long;
And ere yon bells beganne to play,
　　Afar I heard her milking song.'
He looked across the grassy lea,
To right, to left, 'Ho Enderby!'
They rang 'The Brides of Enderby!'

186

With that he cried and beat his breast;
   For lo! along the river's bed
A mighty eygre reared his crest,
   And uppe the Lindis raging sped.
It swept with thunderous noises loud;
Shaped like a curling snow-white cloud,
Or like a demon in a shroud.

And rearing Lindis backward pressed,
   Shook all her trembling bankes amaine;
Then madly at the eygre's breast
   Flung uppe her weltering walls again.
Then bankes came down with ruin and rout—
Then beaten foam flew round about—
Then all the mighty floods were out.

So farre, so fast the eygre drave
   The heart had hardly time to beat,
Before a shallow, seething wave
   Sobbed in the grasses at our feet:
The feet had hardly time to flee
Before it brake against the knee,
And all the world was in the sea.

Upon the roofe we sate that night,
   The noise of bells went sweeping by:
I marked the lofty beacon light
   Stream from the church-tower, red and high—
A lurid mark and dread to see;
And awesome bells they were to me,
That in the dark rang 'Enderby.'

They rang the sailor lads to guide
    From roofe to roofe who fearless rowed;
And I—my sonne was at my side,
    And yet the ruddy beacon glowed:
And yet he moaned beneath his breath,
'O come in life, or come in death!
O lost! my love, Elizabeth.'

And didst thou visit him no more?
    Thou didst, thou didst, my daughter deare!
The waters laid thee at his doore,
    Ere yet the early dawn was clear.
Thy pretty bairns in fast embrace,
The lifted sun shone on thy face,
Downe drifted to thy dwelling-place.

That flow strewed wrecks about the grass,
    That ebbe swept out the flocks to sea;
A fatal ebbe and flow, alas!
    To manye more than myne and mee;
But each will mourn his own (shee sayeth),
And sweeter woman ne'er drew breath
Than my sonne's wife, Elizabeth.

I shall never hear her more
By the reedy Lindis' shore,
'Cusha, Cusha, Cusha!' calling
Ere the early dews be falling;
I shall never hear her song,
'Cusha, Cusha!' all along.
Where the sunny Lindis floweth,
Floweth, floweth;
From the meads where melick groweth,
When the water winding down,
Onward floweth to the town.

I shall never see her more
    Where the reeds and rushes quiver,
    Shiver, quiver;
    Stand beside the sobbing river,
Sobbing, throbbing, in its falling,
To the sandy lonesome shore,
I shall never hear her calling,
    'Leave your meadow grasses mellow,
    Mellow, mellow;
    Quit your cowslips, cowslips yellow;
Come uppe, Whitefoot, come uppe, Lightfoot;
    Quit your pipes of parsley hollow,

    Hollow, hollow:
    Come uppe, Lightfoot, rise and follow;
Lightfoot, Whitefoot,
    From your clovers lift the head;
Come uppe, Jetty, follow, follow,
Jetty to the milking-shed.'

Keith of Ravelston

Sydney Dobell

The murmur of the mourning ghost
    That keeps the shadowy kine:
'O Keith of Ravelston,
    The sorrows of thy line!'

Ravelston, Ravelston,
    The merry path that leads
Down the golden morning hill
    And through the silver meads;

Ravelston, Ravelston,
　The stile beneath the tree,
The maid that kept her mother's kine,
　The song that sang she!

She sang her song, she kept her kine,
　She sat beneath the thorn,
When Andrew Keith of Ravelston
　Rode through the Monday morn.

His henchmen sing, his hawk-bells ring,
　His belted jewels shine;
O Keith of Ravelston,
　The sorrows of thy line!

Year after year, where Andrew came,
　Comes evening down the glade;
And still there sits a moonshine ghost
　Where sat the sunshine maid.

Her misty hair is faint and fair,
　She keeps the shadowy kine;—
O Keith of Ravelston,
　The sorrows of thy line!

I lay my hand upon the stile,
　The stile is lone and cold;
The burnie that goes babbling by
　Says nought that can be told.

Yet, stranger! here, from year to year,
　She keeps her shadowy kine;—
O Keith of Ravelston,
　The sorrows of thy line!

Step out three steps where Andrew stood—
   Why blanch thy cheeks for fear!
The ancient stile is not alone,
   'Tis not the burn I hear!

She makes her immemorial moan,
   She keeps her shadowy kine;—
O Keith of Ravelston,
   The sorrows of thy line!

Annabel Lee

Edgar Allan Poe

It was many and many a year ago,
   In a kingdom by the sea,
That a maiden there lived whom you may know
   By the name of Annabel Lee;
And this maiden she lived with no other thought
   Than to love and be loved by me.

I was a child and she was a child,
   In this kingdom by the sea,
But we loved with a love that was more than love,
   I and my Annabel Lee;
With a love that the winged seraphs of heaven
   Coveted her and me.

And this was the reason that, long ago,
   In this kingdom by the sea,
A wind blew out of a cloud, chilling
   My beautiful Annabel Lee;
So that her highborn kinsmen came
   And bore her away from me,
To shut her up in a sepulchre
   In this kingdom by the sea.

The angels, not half so happy in heaven,
  Went envying her and me;
Yes! that was the reason (as all men know,
  In this kingdom by the sea)
That the wind came out of the cloud one night,
  Chilling and killing my Annabel Lee.

But our love it was stronger by far than the love
  Of those who were older than we,
  Of many far wiser than we;
And neither the angels in heaven above,
  Nor the demons down under the sea,
Can ever dissever my soul from the soul
  Of the beautiful Annabel Lee:

For the moon never beams, without bringing me
    dreams
  Of the beautiful Annabel Lee;
And the stars never rise, but I feel the bright eyes
  Of the beautiful Annabel Lee;
And so, all the night-tide, I lie down by the side
Of my darling—my darling—my life and my bride,
  In the sepulchre there by the sea,
  In her tomb by the sounding sea.

Against Oblivion
Sir Henry Newbolt

Cities drowned in olden time
Keep, they say, a magic chime
Rolling up from far below
When the moon-led waters flow.

So within me, ocean deep,
Lies a sunken world asleep.
Lest its bells forget to ring,
Memory! set the tide a-swing!

Fear no more
William Shakespeare

Fear no more the heat o' the sun,
   Nor the furious winter's rages;
Thou thy worldly task hast done,
   Home art gone, and ta'en thy wages;
Golden lads and girls all must,
As chimney-sweepers, come to dust.

Fear no more the frown o' the great,
   Thou art past the tyrant's stroke:
Care no more to clothe and eat;
   To thee the reed is as the oak:
The sceptre, learning, physic, must
All follow this, and come to dust.

Fear no more the lightning-flash,
   Nor the all-dreaded thunder-stone;
Fear not slander, censure rash;
   Thou hast finished joy and moan:
All lovers young, all lovers must
Consign to thee, and come to dust. . . .

Come unto these Yellow Sands

William Shakespeare

Come unto these yellow sands,
   And then take hands:
Curtsied when you have, and kissed—
   The wild waves whist—
Foot it featly here and there;
And, sweet sprites, the burthen bear.
    Hark, hark!
      Bow-wow!
    The watch-dogs bark:
      Bow-wow!
    Hark, hark! I hear
The strain of strutting Chanticleer
    Cry: *Cock-a-diddle-dow.*

The Old Ships

James Elroy Flecker

I have seen old ships sail like swans asleep
Beyond the village which men still call Tyre,
With leaden age o'ercargoed, dipping deep
For Famagusta and the hidden sun
That rings black Cyprus with a lake of fire;
And all those ships were certainly so old
Who knows how oft with squat and noisy gun,
Questing brown slaves or Syrian oranges,
The pirate Genoese
Hell-raked them till they rolled
Blood, water, fruit and corpses up the hold.
But now through friendly seas they softly run,
Painted the mid-sea blue or shore-sea green,
Still patterned with the vine and grapes in gold.

But I have seen,
Pointing her shapely shadows from the dawn
And image tumbled on a rose-swept bay,
A drowsy ship of some yet older day;
And, wonder's breath indrawn,
Thought I—who knows—who knows—but in that
    same
(Fished up beyond Æœa, patched up new
—Stern painted brighter blue—)
That talkative, bald-headed seaman came
(Twelve patient comrades sweating at the oar)
From Troy's doom-crimson shore,
And with great lies about his wooden horse
Set the crew laughing, and forgot his course.

It was so old a ship—who knows, who knows?
—And yet so beautiful, I watched in vain
To see the mast burst open with a rose,
And the whole deck put on its leaves again.

Drake's Drum

Sir Henry Newbolt

Drake he's in his hammock an' a thousand mile away,
    (Capten, art tha sleepin' there below?),
Slung atween the round shot in Nombre Dios Bay,
    An' dreamin' arl the time o' Plymouth Hoe.
Yarnder lumes the Island, yarnder lie the ships,
    Wi' sailor lads a dancin' heel-an'-toe,
An' the shore-lights flashin', an' the night-tide
    dashin',
    He sees et arl so plainly as he saw et long ago.

Drake he was a Devon man, an' rüled the Devon seas,
  (Capten, art tha sleepin' there below?),
Rovin' tho his death fell, he went wi' heart at ease,
  An' dreamin' arl the time o' Plymouth Hoe.
'Take my drum to England, hang et by the shore,
  Strike et when your powder's runnin' low;
If the Dons sight Devon, I'll quit the port o' Heaven,
  An' drum them up the Channel as we drummed them long
    ago.'

Drake he's in his hammock till the great Armadas come,
  (Capten, art tha sleepin' there below?),
Slung atween the round shot, listenin' for the drum,
  An' dreamin' arl the time o' Plymouth Hoe.
Call him on the deep sea, call him up the Sound,
  Call him when ye sail to meet the foe;
Where the old trade's plyin' an' the old flag flyin'
  They shall find him ware an' wakin', as they found him
    long ago!

Echo Song

Lord Tennyson

The splendour falls on castle walls
  And snowy summits old in story:
The long light shakes across the lakes,
  And the wild cataract leaps in glory.
Blow, bugle, blow, set the wild echoes flying,
Blow, bugle; answer, echoes, dying, dying, dying.

O hark, O hear! how thin and clear,
  And thinner, clearer, farther going!
O sweet and far from cliff and scar
  The horns of Elfland faintly blowing!
Blow, let us hear the purple glens replying:
Blow, bugle; answer, echoes, dying, dying, dying.

O love, they die in yon rich sky,
   They faint on hill or field or river:
Our echoes roll from soul to soul,
   And grow for ever and for ever.
Blow, bugle, blow, set the wild echoes flying,
And answer, echoes, answer, dying, dying, dying.

The Fairy Thorn

Samuel Ferguson

'Get up, our Anna dear, from the weary spinning wheel;
   For your father's on the hill, and your mother is asleep:
Come up above the crags, and we'll dance a highland reel
   Around the fairy thorn on the steep.'

At Anna Grace's door 'twas thus the maidens cried,
   Three merry maidens fair in kirtles of the green;
And Anna laid the rock and the weary wheel aside,
   The fairest of the four, I ween.

They're glancing through the glimmer of the quiet eve,
   Away in milky wavings of neck and ankle bare;
The heavy-sliding stream in its sleepy song they leave,
   And the crags in the ghostly air:

And linking hand and hand, and singing as they go,
   The maids along the hill-side have ta'en their fearless way,
Till they come to where the rowan trees in lonely beauty
     grow
   Beside the Fairy Hawthorn grey.

The hawthorn stands between the ashes tall and slim,
   Like matron with her twin grand-daughters at her knee;
The rowan berries cluster o'er her low head grey and dim
   In ruddy kisses sweet to see.

The merry maidens four have ranged them in a row,
   Between each lovely couple a stately rowan stem,
And away in mazes wavy, like skimming birds they go,
   Oh, never carolled bird like them!

But solemn is the silence of the silvery haze
   That drinks away their voices in echoeless repose,
And dreamily the evening has stilled the haunted braes,
   And dreamier the gloaming grows.

And sinking one by one, like lark-notes from the sky
   When the falcon's shadow saileth across the open shaw,
Are hushed the maidens' voices, as cowering down they lie
   In the flutter of their sudden awe.

For, from the air above, and the grassy ground beneath,
   And from the mountain-ashes and the old Whitethorn
     between,
A power of faint enchantment doth through their beings
     breathe,
   And they sink down together on the green.

They sink together silent, and stealing side to side,
  They fling their lovely arms o'er their drooping necks so
    fair.
Then vainly strive again their naked arms to hide,
  For their shrinking necks again are bare.

Thus clasped and prostrate all, with their heads together
    bowed,
  Soft o'er their bosoms' beating—the only human sound—
They hear the silky footsteps of the silent fairy crowd,
  Like a river in the air, gliding round.

Nor scream can any raise, nor prayer can any say,
  But wild, wild, the terror of the speechless three—
For they feel fair Anna Grace drawn silently away,
  By whom they dare not look to see.

They feel their tresses twine with her parting locks of gold,
  And the curls elastic falling, as her head withdraws;
They feel her sliding arms from their trancèd arms unfold,
  But they dare not look to see the cause:

For heavy on their senses the faint enchantment lies
  Through all that night of anguish and perilous amaze;
And neither fear nor wonder can ope their quivering eyes
  Or their limbs from the cold ground raise.

Till out of Night the Earth has rolled her dewy side,
  With every haunted mountain and streamy vale below;
When, as the mist dissolves in the yellow morning-tide,
  The maidens' trance dissolveth so.

Then fly the ghastly three as swiftly as they may,
  And tell their tale of sorrow to anxious friends in vain—
They pined away and died within the year and day,
  And ne'er was Anna Grace seen again.

La Belle Dame sans Merci

John Keats

'O what can ail thee, knight-at-arms,
　Alone and palely loitering?
The sedge has withered from the lake,
　And no birds sing.

'O what can ail thee, knight-at-arms,
　So haggard and so woe-begone?
The squirrel's granary is full,
　And the harvest's done.

'I see a lily on thy brow
　With anguish moist and fever dew,
And on thy cheeks a fading rose
　Fast withereth too.'

'I met a lady in the meads,
　Full beautiful—a faery's child,
Her hair was long, her foot was light,
　And her eyes were wild.

'I made a garland for her head,
　And bracelets too, and fragrant zone;
She looked at me as she did love,
　And made sweet moan.

'I set her on my pacing steed
　And nothing else saw all day long,
For sidelong would she bend, and sing
　A faery's song.

'She found me roots of relish sweet,
　And honey wild, and manna dew,
And sure in language strange she said—
　"I love thee true."

'She took me to her elfin grot,
    And there she wept, and sighed full sore,
And there I shut her wild wild eyes
    With kisses four.

'And there she lullèd me asleep,
    And there I dreamed—Ah! woe betide!
The latest dream I ever dreamed
    On the cold hill's side.

'I saw pale kings and princes too,
    Pale warriors, death-pale were they all;
They cried—"La Belle Dame sans Merci
    Hath thee in thrall!"

'I saw their starved lips in the gloam,
    With horrid warning gapèd wide,
And I awoke and found me here,
    On the cold hill's side.

'And this is why I sojourn here,
    Alone and palely loitering,
Though the sedge is withered from the lake
    And no birds sing.'

England

E. H. W. Meyerstein

A being stood before me in a dream,
Most like a boy whom I at school had known;
His voice was pitched in a high fearless tone,
And his grey eyes burned with a steady gleam.
The sun had set, but one departing beam
Lingered upon the mass of lichened stone,
'Gainst which my arms were casually thrown,
There on the hillside where he shone supreme.

He said: 'Not love for you, but destiny,
Hath roused me from the dark ant-peopled turf
To tell you that you tread my realm at last.
And you will bear me ever in your eye,
On wood or plain or height or stream or surf,
Until your limbs above my bones are cast.'

Envoy

Matthew, Mark, Luke, and John,
Bless the bed that I lie on!
And blessed guardian-angel keep
Me safe from danger while I sleep!

Notes

[20] THERE WAS A MONKEY

'Clouting' (verse 7) means patching; 'strip' (verse 8) means smoothed out; and the footman who in old days—when 'eat' (i.e. *et*, line 6) was used for eaten—used to run in front of his master's carriage, was also called a 'lackey' (verse 6). This old rhyme doesn't tell us much we didn't know before; but there are nine sharp, clear pictures in it.

[21] THE INKY BOYS

Agrippa used the 'great goose-feather' (line 20) to write with—having sharpened its stalk and split the tip. These pens were called quills, and everybody used them for writing with ink before steel nibs were invented.

[23] THE PIGS

'Deride' (line 7) means, to laugh at; and 'comfits' (line 14) are such sweets as sugar-almonds or any dainty seed or fruit covered with sugar.

[24] THE RAGGED GIRL'S SUNDAY

After which, in the poem, this conceited little prig, who thinks herself so much *much* better than the guttersnipe, gets her lesson; but we can manage to discover that for ourselves!

[25] APPLE-PYE

This old alphabet rhyme, like the two counting-rhymes that follow it, takes us back to the days of our great-great-grandmothers and of *their* grandmothers too. Then I and J were not always thought of as separate *letters*. Nowadays if we wanted to make the alphabet complete we should have to add: I Itched for it, or had an Inch of it, or made himself Ill with it. So again with U and V. There is no V in the second part of the rhyme. 'J joined for it,' means, I fancy, that he joined battle for it, perhaps with F, though he might also have Jigged, Jumped, Jostled or Jabbered for it. Z must have said 'zat' for *.sat*. Ampersy-and (in the last line of all) is the name that is given to the sign &. It was originally spelt &-per-se-and, which means & *by itself means and*; and we still use it in &c., which stands for the Latin 'etcetera,' and means, *and other things*.

By 'fast who will,' E meant that *he'd* have some even if the others decided not to taste the Pie at all—to *fast*: and he said this in three words!

Another way very small children learnt their letters in those old times was by means of a Hornbook. The alphabet, the Lord's Prayer and the digits, 1 to 9, were printed on a piece of thick paper or cardboard, and this was fixed to a piece of wood which was shaped like a battledore, and had a hole in the handle. To keep the cardboard from getting dirty it was covered with a thin strip of transparent *horn*. The handle was threaded with a piece of twine or tape or ribbon, and its owner hung his hornbook round his middle. In this way (if he pleased) he could learn his letters the whole day long!

[30] THE THREE CATS

This rhyme comes from the north of England where all but the 't' in the word *the* is left out in speaking, as in 't'fire.' The three cats are witch cats every one, and a merry time they and the witch's cocks and hens have of it.

[30] BOBBY SHAFTO

'Bonny' means handsome, merry, dearest and good, and 'ain for evermair' is, own for ever more—for always. In Bobby's day men wore breeches with 'silver buckles,' and his yellow hair would come down to his shoulders.

[31] FIVE VERY OLD RIDDLES

The five answers are: a walnut, the teeth, a bramble-blossom (look at one!), a face in a looking-glass, and a star.

[32] THE SPRING WALK

'Flowers' (line 8) is two syllables; 'violets' (line 12) is three.

[33] BROTHER AND SISTER

'Brake' (line 7) means either the bright-green fern-like bracken, or a thicket, which is a little wood whose trees grow very close together.

[34] FULL MOON

Old jingles like this were sung in their games by children ages before they came to be put down in print. But when you learn anything by hearing it said it is easier to make a mistake than when you learn it by reading it. For this reason such jingles went through many changes, and there may be as many as ten different

204

ways of saying such rhymes as 'Sally, Sally Waters' or 'Eena, deena' or 'We are three courtiers out of Spain' in ten different parts of England. 'Cover' (line 8) means 'will be enough for us all.'

[35] A CATCHING SONG
I have marked the words here and there where the beat or accent might be missed; but there is often more than one good way of reading a poem.

[35] THE GARDEN YEAR
'Gillyflowers' (verse 7) here, I think, means carnations; but it sometimes means wallflowers and sometimes the sweet-smelling stock.

[38] HARK!
'Waggletail' is, of course, the pretty, nimble wagtail or Dish-washer or Washerwoman, either pied or grey, or (even more beautiful) yellow. The grey has a curious habit, I have read, of pecking at windows—even when there are no flies! The 'Mavis' is an old name for the song-thrush, so the other 'Thrush' (line 2) must be the missel thrush, who is also called Throstle Cock and Storm Cock, because he will sit whistling away, loud and harsh and wild, on the topmost branch of a high tree in February or March when the wind is roaring round him and the rain pelting down over his head.

[41] WHO KILLED COCK ROBIN?
A 'showl' (verse 5) is a shovel, and a 'link' (verse 9) is a torch—just in case it should get dark, perhaps.

[43] BAD LUCK
'Ye' means you, and 'thrive' means to go on well and with a light heart. 'Never' is a very long time; but I can still remember how miserable I was one fine morning when I was about seven at killing a sparrow. I threw a stone at him as he was bathing in the dust on a sunny road, and as he was a longish way off, it was a mighty good aim. But even that did not comfort me, when I took him up in my hand—with his shut eyes and his clenched claws.

[44] THE BABES IN THE WOOD
'Plight' (line 8) means the danger they were in, as the old story tells.

[46] THE DUKE
Say it with a good thump on every syllable of Cumberland.

[46] A GRACE
Paddocks are frogs; froggies is an old word for cold hands; a
benison is a blessing.

[46] JAMES AND THE SHOULDER OF MUTTON
Jemmy went to the *baker's* to fetch his dinner because in the days
when this rhyme was written this was the custom. The baker
with his great brick oven could bake perhaps three or four dozen
legs and shoulders of mutton or cakes at the same time, and this
saved as many fires. Otherwise, meat-jacks were then in use. You
hung your leg of mutton on a hook attached to a brass cylinder,
and wound up the clockwork inside with a key. This jack hung
in a hood-shaped receptacle made of tin, rather like a very large
bee-hive cut in half. This was put in front of the fire, and the
clockwork kept the joint slowly turning round and round (with
a little *click*)—first one side, then the other—so that it should not
burn. The grease fell into a dripping pan beneath. Before jacks
came into use, short-legged dogs were used to turn a spit on
which the joints were fixed.

Jemmy was rude to the baker's man—and he burned his
fingers, but he had the sense to save all he could when the dish
fell into the kennel, and to change his mind when he saw he had
been in the wrong. This 'kennel' (verse 8) was a water-gutter,
which in Jemmy's day ran down over the stones in the *middle*
of the street. In some towns, as in Cambridge to this day, a
little brook coursed along the main street.

These lessons in rhyme—as this poem or 'The Ant and the
Cricket,' or 'The Pigs,' or 'Tom at Dinner' might be called,
may not have very much *poetry* in them, but how very clearly
you can *see* all that happens in them; in this case, the baker's
man in his white apron, the mutton tumbling along the gutter,
the grinning boys, and Jemmy rushing home, joint in hand, the
broken dish left behind him.

[48] I SAW A SHIP
The 'hold' (line 6) of a ship is the place where the cargo or what
it is laden with is put; and `packet' (last verse) means a wallet or
bag of letters.

[49] LITTLE JACK HORNER

This old story of Jack and his mother—who sang him so many pretty songs or sonnets and lullabies till he learned to sing too—seems to show that he himself made up the well-known nursery rhyme about himself; and an old rhyme it is. Charles Lamb said that the *b* in plumbs made them taste sweeter!

[50] THE FAIRIES

You will find the places mentioned in the third verse in a good-sized map of Ireland, County Donegal, though not perhaps the little men themselves, or even Bridget. The Northern Lights (verse 3) is the name given to a marvellous brilliance that is sometimes seen in the northern skies after dark, and particularly in northern countries. Its streamers of light soar high into the deep, dark air in their many lovely colours—yellow, pale red and deep red. Sometimes these rays seem to be in wild, wavy motion, and they are called the Merry Dancers.

[53] NOW THE DAY IS OVER

'Nigh' (verse 1) means near; 'repose' (verse 3) means sleep; and 'visions' (verse 4) are the happiest, loveliest and most radiant of all dreams.

[54] DAYBREAK

'Chanticleer' (verse 6) (the first of its three syllables pronounced like the word *chant*) is the old French name—meaning *shrill-voice*—of the farm-cock or 'the red cock and the grey' of the ballads, and perhaps the first of all wild things to be tamed by man. He crows at midnight and at dawn, his voice sounding out shrill as the call of a battle-trumpet or 'clarion.' Like Chanticleer for cock, so Bruin is the old name for a bear, Puss for a cat, Reynard for a fox. Birds too have such names as Robin Red-breast, Jack Daw, Mag Pie, Tom Tit.

[55] THE FIRST BEE

Snowdrops, cold and white as the hoar frost, bloom the earliest of all winter flowers; and the first bees of the new year, enticed out of their hives by the first sunbeams, hum about them 'tentatively' or uncertainly, and not with that wonderful low thunder they make—hundreds of them together—in the thick rosy flowers of an apple-tree.

[55] SPRING

The four 'pretty birds' are, I think, the cuckoo, the nightingale whose inward note is more like *yoog* than 'jug,' the greenfinch and the owl. 'Aye' (line 7) means all day long.

[56] THREE CUCKOO RHYMES

The least little pause on the *ins* in this first old rhyme and also on the second syllables of 'April' and of 'August' improves its lilt.

He sings *Cuck-oo*; *she* takes an egg out of some other bird's nest and lays one of her own in its place. She is like a hawk in flight and of a *bright* ash-grey where the light shines on her.

This is from a long poem called 'The Living Spring' by Jane Taylor.

[57] THE GREEN LINNET

'In ecstasies' means beside himself with joy and delight; and 'to hover' (that usually rhymes with lover) means to pause in the air on fluttering wings or (as the kestrel does) on wings all but perfectly still. Hazel leaves seem to twinkle in the least wind, because they are silvery on one side and green on the other.

[57] THE PET LAMB

This is only the beginning of a much longer poem, and a very beautiful one too—with all the faint colours and the quiet of evening. But the rest can easily be found if you wish to read it.

[58] THE SWAN

Although this translation from a very old poem is not in rhyme, it brings to mind a wild swan in its life and beauty more vividly than any other poem I know. 'Welkin,' in the fifth line, means the sky: the wide snow-white wings of the swan stoop and rest upon the strength of the air just as a swimmer rests on the water; and as the great bird speeds on, its plumes faintly 'sing.' So with the waft in the dark of an owl's wings, and the faint *skir* of a swallow or a swift as it skims swishing through the air. 'Bending' (line 4) means curving.

[58] STUPIDITY STREET

This marvellous little poem that says so much in so few words reminds one of the old story of the goose that laid golden eggs, and of what the foolish old woman did with it. I can myself remember, when I was a child, often seeing strings—yes, strings —of dead *skylarks* hanging up in a fishmonger's shop, like coloured paper-chains at Christmas!

208

'Covert' (line 1) means hidden or secret; and 'sac' and 'amang' are Scottish ways of saying *so* and *among*.

[60] THE SPIDER AND THE FLY

She *did* call another day, and alas, came out no more! But the rest of the poem takes rather a long time to say this, so I have made room here instead for *Will you, Won't you*—a rhyme sung by the Gryphon and the Mock Turtle, dancing round with Alice in a ring, in *Alice in Wonderland*. It shows how the same metre as 'The Spider and the Fly'—*tiddy-dùmpty tiddy-dùmpty*—goes with a different kind of chorus—*dùmpty dumpty dumpty dumpty dùmpty dumpty dùm*—though the 'Will you, won't you's' must be said as coaxingly as an old woman at nightfall calls in her cat!

'Will you walk a little faster?' said a whiting to a snail.
'There's a porpoise close behind us, and he's treading on my tail.
See how eàgerly the lobsters and the turtles all advance!
They are waiting on the shingle—will you come and join the
    dance?
  Will you, wòn't you, will you, won't you, will you join the
    dance?
  Will you, won't you, will you, won't you, won't you join the
    dance?

'You can really have no notion how delightful it will be,
When they take us up and throw us, with the lobsters, out to
    sea!'
But the snail replied 'Too far, too far!' and gave a look askance—
Said he thanked the whiting kindly, but he would not join the
    dance:
  Would not, could not, would not, could not, would not join
    the dance.
  Would not, could not, would not, could not, could not join
    the dance.

'What matters it how far we go?' his scaly friend replied.
'There is another shore, you know, upon the other side.
The farther off from England the nearer is to France—
Then turn not pale, beloved snail, but come and join the dance.

Will you, won't you, will you, won't you, will you join the
dance?
Will you, won't you, will you, won't you, won't you join the
dance?'

Lewis Carroll

[62] FOR A DEWDROP

When a drop of dew lies trembling on a thorn in the sun it
seems to have trapped or 'snared' in its one lovely crystal bead
of water reflections not only of all the colours of the rainbow but
of everything around it. Look close into one and see for yourself.

[62] PRECIOUS STONES

In old days, before matches came into use, you got a light by
snapping a *flint*-spark into powdery wood-dust or tinder, and
blowing it into a flame. With this you lit your farthing-dip or
tallow candle.

[63] THE CHILD AND THE SNAKE

This poem rather jolts along, but how well it tells its queer little
story—of how Henry, who (as he is called an infant) cannot be
more than four or five, used to run off with his breakfast mess
or bowl of bread and milk, and share it with a viper which he
describes to his mother as a fine grey *bird*, and calls Grey Pate
(or Grey Head or Grey Nob) when, with a tap of his spoon, he
means to make it mind its manners! It is 'a frightful guest'
because but one prick of its 'envenomed' or poisonous fangs
might kill him, though if it had been a green or grass snake it
would have been harmless. But as Henry has no fear of it, and his
mother gives it no cause for fear itself, all is well. The word
'wound' (line 28) was once a good rhyme to 'sound,' and
'familiar mate' means a close friend.

[65] FOUR-PAWS

There are many other poems about cats, which in old days
were so valuable that the king himself decreed the prices of them,
according to size and age. There is, for example, the old Irish
monk's poem about his cat called Pangur; there is Gray's
poem about Selima and the bowl of goldfish; and there is Mr.
Harold Monro's—which describes so vividly what a cat does,
and even *feels* like, when saucer-of-milk-time comes round that
in reading it one almost becomes a cat oneself. *Here* we have two

cats—the prowling old grey mother farm cat who all her life has had to fend for herself and get her food where she can find it —a field mouse in the corn or a rat in the barn—and Four-Paws, her kitten. *He* has a snug home—the little cottage in the lane with its snapdragons and sweet-williams—and a kind, small mistress called Betsy-Jane. *She* roves the stackyard and sleeps in the straw. But she cannot forget him, nor he her; and when twilight falls (and Betsy-Jane's abed) she mews for her son under the window and brings him the 'dark maternal'—the secret motherly—dainties she has been saving for him. 'Shrewdly' (verse 6) means softly, nimbly and cautiously; 'plaintive' means sweet and mournful. I have myself seen a cat leap up clean from the floor on to the shelf of a chimney-piece full of china ornaments and walk from one end of it to the other without so much as touching a single one—even with his back paws! Watch a kitten playing with a walnut or a ball of wool—that's how a poet tries to use words.

[66] THE IRISH HARPER

In line 14 he is speaking of himself, of course, when he says Pat. 'My wallet was scant' (verse 5) means that the bag which the old blind harper carried never had much to eat in it. 'I remembered his case' (verse 5) means that he remembered poor Tray's condition—that he was as hungry and cold as himself. In the third line after that, the slight break in the metre caused by the extra word 'sad' seems to make it *sound* more sorrowful; and so with the 'more' in the last line.

[68] LONE DOG

Look how full *inside* of rhymes this is, and how it seems to give you the very movements—sudden, snarling and thief-like—of the dog that won't have any master but himself. And you love him for it in spite of all his badness and madness. Like all the great adventurers—Dick Whittington, Drake and Columbus and Magellan—he has 'the hunger of the quest'—the longing to dare the dangerous.

[69] THE WOODMAN'S DOG

A 'lurcher' is part collie, part greyhound—the sort of dog often used by poachers.

[70] AS I WALKED

'Repartee' means a quick and ready reply, a kind of tit for tat.

[70] THERE WAS A LADY
Quoth (rhyming with both) is an old word for *said*.

[71] A TRAGIC STORY
A sage is a very wise old man. In this 'curious case' he was an old
Chinaman, but as very wise old men in England don't wear
pigtails, you don't often catch them dancing round and round
and round and round. To 'muse' means to think long and softly
to oneself.

A nonsense story I never tired of when I was eight or nine
was called *Sir Gammer Vans*. It begins like this:

Last Sunday morning at six o'clock in the evening as I
was sailing over the tops of the mountains in my little boat, I
met two men on horseback riding on one mare: so I asked
them, 'Could they tell me whether the little old woman was
dead yet who was hanged last Saturday week for drowning
herself in a shower of feathers?' They said they could not
positively inform me, but if I went to Sir Gammer Vans he
could tell me all about it. 'But how am I to know the house?'
said I. 'Ho, 'tis easy enough,' said they, 'for 'tis a brick house,
built entirely of flints, standing alone by itself in the middle of
sixty or seventy others just like it.' 'Oh, nothing in the world
is easier,' said I. 'Nothing *can* be easier,' said they: so I went on
my way. Now this Sir Gammer Vans was a giant, and bottle-
maker. And as all giants who *are* bottle-makers usually pop
out of a little thumb-bottle from behind the door, so did Sir
Gammer. 'How d'ye do?' says he. 'Very well, I thank you,'
says I. So he gave me a slice of beer, and a cup of cold veal;
and there was a little dog under the table that picked up all the
crumbs. . . .

[72] A MAN OF WORDS
Not much *meaning*, perhaps; but what vivid and lively pictures!

[73] YER'S TU THEE
And here it is in ordinary English:

Here's to you, old apple-tree,
Be sure you bud, be sure you blow,
And bring forth apples good enow [enough],
Hats full! Caps full!
Three-bushel bags full,

Pockets full and all!
          Hurrah! Hurrah!
Oh, yes, hats full, caps full,
And three-bushel bags full,
          Hurrah! Hurrah!

[73] CALM
'That leisurely it blew' means, so slowly and softly it blew.

[73] SIGNS OF RAIN
Some of these 'signs' come before rain in June and some come
with the rain; some, like 'Old Betty's' aching knuckle-joints and
the whirling wind, just before rain, and some, like the faint halo
or rainbow round the moon, as much as two or three days before.
Apart from this 'weather-lore,' the poem is full of vivid glimpses
of a host of interesting things, both indoors and out. The
shepherd (line 7) having seen the haloed moon, 'bodes' or
foresees the long wet days he will spend with his sheep. The
'squalid' toad means earth-coloured, I think. You often see
rooks gliding like 'kites' across the sky, and falling 'precipitate'
or suddenly, just as do the pigeons called *tumblers*. And the drop
is so sudden it is as if they felt the 'piercing ball' shot from the
sportsman's gun.

[74] THE KITE
The last line must be read very carefully to get its full effect.

[76] THE HUNT IS UP
'Harry' is Henry VIII, who in his young days was as nimble and
strong as he was clever, and a fine player of tennis. The deer or
stag is 'at bay' when it is surrounded by the barking dogs.
'Treen' (verse 3) is an old plural of tree, and the '*hey tantara*'
(verse 4) is an imitation of the brassy notes of his huntsmen's
horns.

[77] A-HUNTING WE WILL GO
'Jovial' (verse 5) means loud and jolly; 'embrace' (verse 7)
means welcome both into your arms; and you will find 'Sly
Reynard' off on a little hunting of his own in the next rhyme.

[78] EE-OH!
The word 'lugs' (verse 3) means ears, and comes from the North
of England. The fact that the word 'town' here means a farm-
stead with its farmhouse, barns, byres and pigsty, enclosed by a

213

wall, shows how old this old song is. Nowadays, of course, it means any large collection of buildings—churches, houses, shops and so on, with their streets—which is too big to be called a village and is not a city. A rookery is a sort of rook-town; a mousery a sort of mouse-town. A city is a large town that has been *made* a city by the king. In England it frequently has a cathedral in it, and in the cathedral is the throne of its bishop. But this is a long way from the old fox and his wife.

[79] THE LINCOLNSHIRE POACHER
Lincoln*sheer* (line 1); 'his deer' (last verse) means his small game, rabbits, pheasants, etc. I wish the rollicking old tune of this could have been printed here too.

[80] THE WHITE OWL
A 'roundelay' is a short song and particularly a song that repeats some of itself, as this rhyme does in the last two lines of each verse. Get up early enough and you'll see the cats come stealing home; while as for the *cock-a-diddle-doo's*, they shout across from roost to roost and farm to farm, answering one the other in the hush of daybreak, clean across England from sea to sea!

[81] ONCE I WAS A MONARCH'S DAUGHTER
This refers to the old story of the wicked princess who was changed into an owl, and there is a similar legend of the baker's daughter, who when one afternoon Christ came asking for bread, reproved her mother for making Him so large a loaf. *Hoo, hoo!* she cried—and so has cried ever since.

[82] THE SOUND OF A GUN
The last line doesn't mean that the man with the gun jeers and laughs at the living things he kills—and since a fox is generally 'grinning,' nobody could say that even *he* does that! It means that he shoots them merely to amuse himself. And what goes before in the poem points out, and in the best of spirits, the difference between killing for food and killing for pleasure. What a pretty piece of mockery at the man with the gun is that line about chimney sweeping! But there is no mockery in the next poem. The writer of it, who loves all living things, *burns* with rage at the evil things man does to them.

[83] THE OLD FRIAR REMEMBERS

'Quoir' is an old spelling of choir, and the *matin* bell calls the monks to prayer at dawn or dew-time, when they 'tell their beads,' each bead on the long string they wear being a reminder of one particular prayer.

[83] ELEGY WRITTEN IN A COUNTRY CHURCHYARD

These are only the first three verses of one of the best-known poems in English, and all the solemn quiet and loneliness of the last of evening is in them—that hour while yet the full moon gives only a faint golden light. Indeed, the stillness of the departing day is made to seem even more solemn and intense by the sound of the curfew bell (which in time long gone by was the signal to bid people put out their fires), by the droning of the beetle or cockchafer and the far-off tinkling of the sheep-bells. And how exactly the words in line 7 describe the beetle's flight.

[84] O LADY MOON

In other (much duller) words, if you look at the moon when her horns are pointing to your left she is a new or 'increasing' or *waxing* moon. If they point to the right she is a *waning* moon, and is dwindling to her 'rest.'

[85] THE NEW MOON

'To mark' (line 3) means not only to see but also to notice.

[85] LUCY GRAY, OR SOLITUDE

The fourth verse goes back to the time *before* Lucy Gray was lost. 'Hook' (verse 6) means a knife for chopping up wood for a fire, the 'fagot-brands;' 'blithe' (verse 7) means gentle and nimble—like the mountain roe or deer; and the next three lines mean that Lucy ran on so fast and light-heartedly to meet her mother that the thin frozen snow rose up in the wind like a trail of smoke behind her. But the storm broke—wild wind and bewildering snow. She lost her way; and the dark night came down.

[88] MY PLAYMATE

'Kith and kin' (verse 4) means those near and dear to her; and the shy, bashful boy (verse 4) who loves her, tends her father's cows or 'kine.' The fifth stanza means that the years are 'constant' or unchanging in the way they bring back the seasons— spring, summer, autumn, winter; telling them over or making count of them as a shepherd counts his sheep. The oriole is a

215

lovely, bright-yellow aureole or *golden* bird with a black tail, but it is very rarely seen in England now.

[91] UP IN THE MORNING EARLY

'No' (line 1) is *not*, and 'fare but sparely' means that, their fields being hidden in drifting snow and their pools frozen over with ice, the birds can find very little food. With feathers puffed out to keep them as warm as they can against the keen winter wind, they sit faintly and sadly chirping and shivering or 'chittering' on the bare thorn-tree. 'Frae' means from.

[92] WUL 'E PLAIZE

This is how this very old song—which after cantering along like a colt over a green field suddenly begins to bump along like a hay-cart—is sung by boys in *Devonshire* as they tramp round with their guy on Guy Fawkes' Day. 'Contrive' (line 8) means to plot. In ordinary English it is:

> Will you please to remember
> The fifth of November
> The gunpowder treason and plot:
> I don't see no reason
> Why gunpowder treason
> Should ever be forgot.
> *Guy Fawkes, Guy!*
> He and his companions did contrive
> To blow all England up alive,
> With a dark lantern and a match,
> By God's mercy he was catched.
> *Guy Fawkes, Guy!*

[92] WASSAIL SONG

Wassail (which rhymes with throstle) is a very old word meaning 'All hail to you!'—may you keep hearty, happy and *whole*; and this is a song for children going from door to door singing everybody a Merry Christmas—with an orange and a mince-pie to follow, to keep their voices sweet.

[95] BEAUTIFUL SOUP

This rhyme should be sung—with plenty of expression, especially on the *beau-ootiful*—to the tune of 'Star of the Evening.' It is one of the shorter rhymes out of *Alice in Wonderland*, and the next is a long one out of *Alice Through the Looking-Glass.* Both books were written by Lewis Carroll, and there are very few books I should be sorrier never to have read. If you look through a little piece of cut glass or a lustre you will not only see tiny rainbows everywhere, but everything in the world looks different—just as the queerest things in a dream may be *like* what you see every day, and yet—not like. There the cow jumps over the moon and the little dog laughs to see the sport, and it is just what you expect them to do and wish they did a little oftener.

Alice's world is this sort of topsy-turvy dream-world, where anything may happen at any moment; and the feast of *The Walrus and the Carpenter* is one of the happenings. It is what is *called* nonsense; but if any one should ask what nonsense *is*— well, as with the little pitter-pattering oysters after the feast was over—answer there is none!

[95] THE WALRUS AND THE CARPENTER

Every time I read this rhyme again, I marvel more and more at the skill and the art with which it has been made. In the ever-changing lilt of the lines the words fall as neatly into their places as acorns in their cups. And apart from all the fun and jollity (and the Walrus is so extremely good at 'changing a conversation'!), what a beautiful view it is over those wide sands and that smooth, bright sea; bright indeed!—with both sun and moon to help.

[99] THE DESSERT

In this poem a little girl named Carolina has come down in her best white muslin frock as a special favour to dessert with her father and mother. First, like a robin on a wall, she drops a little curtsy to her elders, as was the custom in the days when the poem was written, and then she is compared to everything on the table. She will have to look in the glass to *see* if her lips are like strawberries; and in the last two lines it is the cake that is 'bedecked' with comfits and sugar-plums and tinsel, not Carolina. A *very* slight accent on the 'with' of the first line tells how the verses should run. Don't stay too long on the last word in line 12. Sloes are the little black berries of the blackthorn that wears so delicate a lace of flowers in very early spring. They are common enough, but very lovely with their faint bluish bloom on them; though not quite such beautiful things as cherries, perhaps, or dangles of red currants with the sun shining through them. Their taste is so bitter that your teeth remember it an hour afterwards.

Mary Lamb, who wrote these lines, was the sister of Charles Lamb, one of the best loved of all English authors. Together they wrote *Tales from Shakespeare* and other books for children, were very fond of one another, and lived together for many years. Mary Lamb died in 1847—an old woman of eighty-three—thirteen years after her brother. It was Charles who thought it is much better when we are young to read old tales and old rhymes than merely to cram ourselves with geography and 'natural history'. They both of them understood what it is to be young, because they so vividly remembered being young themselves. So did Thomas Hood, as the next poem will show.

[100] I REMEMBER
If you hold up a flower, such as a violet, a snowdrop or a narcissus, between your eyes and the sun (without letting them be dazzled by the sun itself) it is so transparent that it is almost as if it *were* 'made of light.' And some flowers even in the dark, when there is no moon in the sky, glow faintly as if with a radiance of their own.

[101] TOM AT DINNER
'Wagging a chin' (line 4) means busily eating. 'Jovially' (last line) here means not loud and jolly but merrily and happily. If this rhyme had been written nowadays the 'smoaking' (verse 2) would be smoking, the 'teaze' tease; and the 'was' (line 13) would be were.

[102] A TRUE STORY
Ann Taylor and her sister, Jane, wrote a great many poems, especially *for* children. Their first book of these was printed in 1804. They wrote them at a time when it was supposed that if you make up a rhyme to please a child it must also teach a lesson. They thought, therefore, that if their rhymes were not only to be clear and simple, but to teach lessons, they must be kept plain and not be too fanciful or imaginative. And so, perhaps—unlike William Blake whose *Songs* that were also meant for children are all light and music and imagination, and a 'joy to hear'— they stopped short when they might have gone a little further. Both sisters, however, quite apart from their skill and care in the use of words, loved to be gay and happy and to make others so, and were really and truly fond of young people. They must,

too, have found a great deal of pleasure in making up rhymes, not only about the good ones, but about the naughty ones also.

Indeed, to judge from their poems, bad children in their day must have been as common as blackberries—greedy, gluttonous, idle, mischievous, cruel, cantankerous, destructive, silly, vain, proud, contemptuous, stubborn, morose, disobedient, dirty and dull. And their rhymes show what all that leads to! But to set them off, there were also little angels of good and sweet behaviour whom Ann and Jane yet managed to make not only natural, but pleasant and likeable in their poems.

Apart from those written by Jane and Ann, a few of the poems in their books were by a friend, called Adelaide O'Keeffe, and she it was who discovered the 'too Good Child':

> 'Oh, pray come in,
>   Mamma's within,
>   Pray do not stay out there,
>   It pours with rain,
>   I say again
>   Come in, and take a chair.'
> Thus lisped little Peggy, whilst holding the door,
> To a poor ragged woman she'd ne'er seen before!

Three muddy, soaking, ravenous and extremely grubby children follow this ragged stranger into Mamma's best parlour, and at last Mamma herself comes down to find it packed with them! She makes the best of things, gives her visitors some food and some old clothes, and then:

> The woman thanked the lady kind,
>   And gratefully went out,
> But Peggy could not comprehend,
>   What this was all about!
> 'Why, dear mamma, was I not right,
>   To ask them in to stay all night?'
> 'My child, your heart is understood;
>   (How can I well explain!)
> When indiscreet—we're call'd TOO GOOD.
>   Never do so again.'

Neither Jane nor Ann Taylor, nor their friend Adelaide,

either—at least in their books—ever allowed her heart to *run away* with her head, or her fancy to bolt off with her good sense; and so their rhymes are all of them very well worth reading when the chance comes. In some ways indeed they are the best poems ever written especially for children.

Cavendish Square (line 4 in the poem, 'A True Story') is still to be found where Ann and her mother found it, though the statue of William, Duke of Cumberland (who won the battle of Culloden) on his gilded leaden horse is now gone, and the *live* prancing horses, the footmen in their wigs and velvet, and the splendid chariots or carriages 'all covered with varnish and gold' which they saw on their walk are gone too. Very seldom nowadays either will a ragged and starving child be seen begging there. 'Grievous complaint' (stanza 12) means the words this little girl sobbed out, being so hungry and wretched. I don't mean that we haven't plenty of other bad things to be ashamed of, only that children are better cared for than they used to be.

Not that this alters the lessons Ann Taylor wished to teach in this 'true story'—first, that having a lot of money is not the same thing as being happy; next, that, quite apart from money, and however much we may grumble, we all of us have a great deal to be thankful for—tongues, for example, to grumble *with*; and last, that (unlike her little beggar girl), most of us have a great deal more than we could honestly say we deserve.

There is one question, however, which always comes back to me when I read this particular poem. Did either the little girl or her mother *give* anything to the beggar child? A penny? A bun? A good meal and a woollen petticoat? About that there's not a word.

If, however, Ann *did* give her a sixpence or a threepenny bit, and gave it in a proud scornful way, then the next poem, 'Self-comforted,' tells you what the little beggar girl might have thought of her. *What* one gives is much, *how* one gives it is much more. Anyhow, a smile *with* a bun enormously sweetens its sugar.

Self-comforted

The ragged child across the street
Stared at the child that looked so sweet.

220

'I'll have a whiter dress than you,
And wear some prettier rose-buds, too;

'And not be proud a bit,' she said,
'I thank you, miss—when I am dead.'
Sara M. B. Piatt

[104] O SWEET CONTENT!

And this means (in much duller words) that it is better to sleep
and dream in peace and to be quiet in your mind than merely to
hoard up bags of money that cannot *buy* either dream or quiet.
And I believe that real hard work, if you love the doing of it, is
not only *like* someone with 'a lovely face,' but will improve your
own looks too!

[105] O HAPPY

'Sufficeth' means, is enough.

[105] ALICE FELL

In this poem, I think, William Wordsworth was telling of
something that had actually happened to him, and had so much
touched his heart that he could not forget it. Before the railways
came into England travellers on long journeys went on foot or
by coach, or, as Wordsworth did, on this occasion, by chaise;
and a chaise was an open, four-wheeled travelling carriage with
two horses, driven by a post-boy sitting on one of their backs,
and sometimes 'with fierce career' (verse 1), that is, very fast.
The carriage being open, he hears the 'piteous moan' of the
little girl sitting hidden behind him in the dark on a little sort of
platform where luggage might be put. She is crying her heart
out because her cloak has somehow been caught between 'the
nave' or middle of one of the wheels, and one of its spokes—the
pieces of wood that are fixed like the rays of a star round its
nave—and is entangled so closely that not even Wordsworth
himself, the post-boy and the little girl together, could pull it
out. The loss of it is a terrible grief to Alice. She is 'insensible to
all relief'—cannot be comforted—not only because her cloak is
now in filthy rags, but her father and mother being dead, there
is nobody, she thinks, to buy her another. So *Wordsworth* did—
and a cloak of very good cloth too, made of wool, and warm,
and one that would stand all sorts of weather.

One of the things that I always particularly enjoy in this poem is the name of the little girl, Alice Fell. The very sound of it seems to help to make you realise how solitary and miserable she was, and even to see her small pale face and bright blue eyes— if that is not taking names too far!

A friend of mine told me that he once saw a little thin mite of a child feasting her eyes on a dressed-up doll in a little old shop window. He went into the shop, bought it and put it in her arms. He said he had never seen a face change so much. It was as if a light from inside had shone out on the outside. It was such a joy to her to have the doll for her own that she could not speak. She merely *looked* and ran away. And that, I should think, is how Alice Fell looked when Wordsworth gave her the cloak.

[107] THE CHIMNEY SWEEPER

In the days of big open chimneys and log fires the chimney sweeps used to take little boys out with them when, with their brushes and soot bags, they went about their work in the early mornings—not only in summer, but in winter too when it was pitch dark, except for the starlight. These small 'sweeps' were perhaps not more than eight or nine years old and some of them had been *sold* to their masters. And however kind many of those masters might be, others were harsh and brutal. To shuffle and clamber up the bricks purposely left sticking out inside the suffocating chimneys, sweeping and scraping the grimy walls as they went, was very hard and very dangerous work. White-haired—that white, close hair with a very little yellow in it, like straw—white-haired little Tom Dacre had been sold to a sweep by *his* father after his mother died; so he was more miserable than the others, but he was comforted by his dream.

[108] THE REVERIE OF POOR SUSAN

A reverie is a day-dream. 'Poor Susan' very early—'in the silence of morning'—is going to her work through the stony city streets of London, and suddenly, as she walks along, she hears a thrush—itself as far away from home as she is—singing over her head. At the sweet loud sound of its voice from out of its cage she trembles with joy—she is 'enchanted.' It carries her back in a day-dream—far, far away to the 'house where she was born'—to the small lonely cottage in its green fields by the misty river, with its trees and its mountains, where in days gone by she used to go out to milk the cows. So clear and vivid is this memory that it blots out for a moment everything around her. It is as if Cheapside had itself become the valley of the home she loves. Then in a moment the thrush is silent; the dream vanishes; hill and stream fade out of her mind. Their 'colours have all passed away from her eyes.'

[109] JOCK O' HAZELDEAN

The first three verses of this Scottish ballad tell how the father of the young man whom this young, bright and beautiful 'ladye' is being made to marry tries and tries to persuade her to dry her tears, and be happy again. 'Why weep ye by the tide?' he asks her, which means either by the shore of the sea or river, or 'why do you still sit weeping here now?' My son, he says, is lord of Langley-dale. He is rich and brave and proud; he will give you gold chains and fine clothes to wear, a 'mettled' or spirited hound, a 'managed' or well-trained hawk, a small, beautiful saddle-horse or 'palfrey' to ride on. But all he says is in vain. She loves only her Jock or Jack of Hazeldean, and nothing but that matters.

At last comes the day fixed for her wedding. The candles are lit in the 'kirk' or church, and all the fine folk are waiting to see the bride. At last they send to seek her, by bower and hall, indoors and out. She is nowhere to be found. She has met her beloved Jock in secret, and having sprung up behind him on to his saddle, has galloped away with him and is now safe over the border.

'O'' is of; 'doon fa'' means fall down; 'loot' means let; 'ha'' is hall, and 'baith' is both.

[110] THE SAILOR'S WIFE

This lively headlong poem about a sailor coming home again from sea to his wife and children is *full* of joy and happiness and life and action. The Scots words may make it difficult at first; but it's well worth all the trouble. The sailor's wife can hardly speak, she is so excited, 'downright dizzy,' at the news. She is almost 'greeting' or crying for joy. Everything is to be put aside to welcome him.

Nobody is to work any more, except to get ready the house. The young girls, the 'jades,' are told to stop their spinning, to sweep up the hearth, to put on the biggest pot, 'the muckle pot,' to dress the children in their best Sunday clothes, to wring or 'thraw' the necks of the two fat hens that have been fed up for this great day, to spread the table, and to make everything look gay and bright and shining—'gar ilka thing look braw.' When she has told everybody what is to be done to welcome the gudeman, she herself runs upstairs to put on her best blue stockings, her Turkey slippers, her fine blue cap or hood or 'bigonet,' and her gown made of the richest lawn and satin. Then off she goes down to the cobbled quay by the water-side to meet him and be clasped in his arms the very moment he steps ashore. 'Caller' (verse 5) means fresh and sweet, and 'aboon the lave' (verse 6) means above all the rest of the world.

[112] THE PIPER

As you can make a pipe to make music with out of a hollow elder stem, or even out of a straw, so you can make a pen out of a 'reed' from a pond, and by 'staining' the clear water make coloured ink to write with. When William Blake was a child he saw in a vision a tree as full of angels as a bush is full of wild roses. So he saw this child 'on a cloud.' And his song is as full of light and happiness as a waterfall is full of bubbles.

[113] OVER HILL, OVER DALE

This is a song sung by a fairy, in answer to a question by Puck, the messenger of the fairy king, in a play—all merriment and moonshine—called *A Midsummer Night's Dream*. 'Thorough' (two syllables) is an old spelling of through—as in 'thoroughfare,' which means a place which you can fare or go *through*; and 'moones' (moon's) is two syllables also. See if you can find out the meaning of any other words you are not *sure* of— 'pale,' for example, means a fence.

[113] EVENING SONG

'To thicken' here means to darken.

[115] A NEW YEAR CAROL

Boys and girls used to sing this ancient carol from house to house at the coming in of the New Year. It is now uncertain what some of it means, though it is as pleasant a thing as ever to *say*.

[116] MERRY ARE THE BELLS AND MERRY WOULD THEY RING

'Gait' means walk—the way your feet go, one after the other;

and 'hollow' means either full of holes or that the legs inside
your hose or stockings are so lean and scranky that there is
plenty of space left! But anyhow, there's always more rhyme
than reason in most of these merry old jingles. And they remind
us as we grow older of—

The days we went a-gipsying a long time ago,
When lads and lasses in their best were dressed from top to toe,
When hearts were light and faces bright, nor thought of care
    or woe,
In the days we went a-gipsying a long time ago.

[117] DANCE!
[117] BO PEEPER
[118] HERE SITS

These last three rhymes are old finger and face rhymes. The first
is a finger rhyme—Foreman, Middleman, Ringman and
Littleman being old names for the four fingers, or, as they are
called in Essex, Bess Bumpkin, Bill Wilkin, Long Linkin, and
Little Dick.

You say 'Bo Peeper' (the second rhyme), to a baby, touching
with the very tip of your finger first its eyes, then its nose, chin,
tooth, tongue and mouth, one to every line. The same with
'*Here sits*.' The Lord Mayor is the forehead, his two men are the
eyes, then right cheek, left cheek, tip of nose, mouth and chin.
Or, for a still shorter rhyme—just gently sliding one finger down
from top to tip of the small nose—there is this:

My mother and your mother
    Went over the way;
Said my mother to your mother,
    'It's chop-a-nose day!'

[118] THE SILLY
There were sillies even as far back as the reign of Richard II;
and it was in his reign that this old rhyme was made.

[119] THE PRIEST AND THE MULBERRY TREE
Line 15 means, he said *Whoa*, and his mare stopped; 'docile'
means, easily managed; and line 26 (last stanza) means that the
good old priest said out loud what (standing up there on his
saddle) he was a little fondly or foolishly thinking to himself:

> If you your lips would keep from slips,
> Five things observe with care;
> *To* whom you speak, *of* whom you speak,
> And *how*, and *when* and *where*.

[120] THE BOYS AND THE APPLE-TREE

The old 'man-traps' (verse 10) which were set to catch 'in-truders,' robbers and trespassers were like enormous rat-traps with a very powerful spring and rows of 'terrible teeth' like a shark. They were hidden in the long grass or weeds of a wood or an orchard, so that not a glint showed at night and very little by day. At touch of prowling foot on the little iron plate in the middle, the teeth sprang up with such force that they nearly met in the trespasser's leg. And there, poor wretch, he stayed, caught like a miserable rabbit, until someone came to release him. 'In awe' means in fear and dread.

The three boys in the rhymes *talk* like little boys in an old-fashioned book, but what they say is very good sense for all that.

[122] THE TRUE STORY OF WEB-SPINNER

What is most curious about this poem is how, in reading it, it seems to be about an extremely wicked and merciless old miser whose whole house is a kind of man-trap, and yet you know all the time he is only a spider.

'Visage' (line 5) means face. 'Felon' (line 6) means a wicked wretch; 'averred' (line 18) means said truly; 'troth' (line 36) means truth; 'privily' (line 17 from end) means secretly; 'churl,' a surly miser; and 'caitiff' even worse.

[126] LITTLE BILLEE

When little Billee 'went up' (in line 25), he climbed almost as high as he could get on a ship (see 'On a Friday Morn,' page 130), and if you want to say where he got to as sailors say it, you must leave out the 'p' in 'top,' and come down sharply on the 'gal'—*to'Gal't*.

There is another comical poem about hardship at sea—*this* kind of hardship, I mean—which is called 'The Yarn of the *Nancy Bell*,' but I don't think Billee had anything to do with it, and fat Jack couldn't have. 'A Seventy-three' is a battleship of seventy-three guns.

[127] SAILOR AND TAILOR

'Baith' (line 2) means both; 'Cloot' (line 6) means cloth—and the tailor is sewing up the seam of a jacket or of a pair of breeches. I am not sure what 'cast his jacket' (verse 4) means, but 'a fancy man' is a sweetheart, and if he has a curly pow or head, then he is a curly-headed sweetheart. 'Planestanes' (verse 5) means flagstones. 'He daurna brack' (verse 6) means he—the *tailor* lad—dares not break.

[128] THE SAILOR'S CONSOLATION
'Slewed his quid' (line 3) means that Barney shifted the tobacco he was chewing from one cheek into the other. Both these two old sailors are laughing at timid 'landsmen' who fear and hate the sea—except from the shore!

[129] BLACK-EYED SUSAN
'Streamers' (line 2) are long flags or pennons flying in the wind from the mast-top of ships of battle; 'yard' (line 7) is a cross-piece of wood or timber fixed high up on a mast to hold a sail; 'pinions' are wings. William slid down a rope to his Susan because it was the quickest way, though it burnt his hands.

[130] ON A FRIDAY MORN
It's bad luck to a sailor to sail on a Friday, and it's worse luck for him to see a mermaid combing her yellow hair as she sits, looking-glass in hand, on the rocks. Sure enough, as soon as this ship was out to sea, a storm rose, and the 'sailor-boys' went climbing up 'into the top'—a little platform at the mast-head—to reef or fold in the sails, while the landsmen or 'land-lubbers' lay groaning and sea-sick down below. But all in vain, the storm-driven seas were so rough that they had washed away (verse 4) the ship's boat long before she herself went three times round and sunk to the bottom of the sea.

[131] THE ANCIENT MARINER
These few stanzas are from a very long poem telling of a marvellous voyage—tempest and mist and ice, dead calm and tropic heat, and the solitude of great oceans. I wish there were space for *all* of it. Here the first five stanzas describe the water-snakes this old sailor saw playing in shadow at the ship's side under the radiance of the moon; the last four describe the sweet sounds of the chant of a troop of spirits haunting the becalmed and lonely ship.

[133] THE SHIP
This is a poem that tells of 'the patient bravery of a ship that has

not been fighting, nor making money by trade or commerce, but has been through trouble and makes no boast of it.'

[134] THE 'SHANNON' AND THE 'CHESAPEAKE'

Though this old story in rhyme of the famous fight on June 1st, 1813, between these two frigates or ships-of-war, the English and the American, may sound a little boastful here and there, it doesn't tell us that the *Shannon* only had 38 guns to the *Chesapeake*'s 49; but it does tell us, and truthfully too, that the English flag went up to the top of the *Chesapeake*'s mast only fifteen minutes after the 'dreadful duel' began. But many brave men were killed, including the 'noble captain' of the *Chesapeake*, and many, like Captain Broke himself, were wounded; and this is the *misery* of war.

'Tars' (verse 3) is short for Jack Tarpaulins, a nickname for sailors, who used in the old days, too, to tar the pigtails in which they wore their long hair to keep it neat and tidy. 'Within hail' (verse 4) means that the two ships had drawn so close together that a man could be heard and understood shouting from one to the other.

[136] THE OLD NAVY

A 'carronade' (line 1) is a big ship's gun. 'I haven't the gift of the gab' means I'm not much good at speechifying, or I'm better at *doing* than at wagging my tongue; and line 6 means that this tough old sea captain had fought his ship against ships far stronger than she—and had always won!

[137] MEN WHO MARCH AWAY

In March, 1805, Napoleon—'Old Boney'—threatened to bring his soldiers across the sea from France and to invade England. The English all along the coast got ready for him, and this song is a marching song for them; but Old Boney never came! Make up a tune to it if you can, with *Right fol-fol* for a sounding chorus.

[138] TOM BOWLING

There are six words at least in this lament for Tom Bowling that come—as he did—from the sea. 'A sheer hulk,' for example, is a wreck with all her masts gone; and Tom, poor soul, is dead. A ship is 'broached to' when her sails are set or 'laid aback,' so that (for a time) she wallows helplessly in the waves; and Tom's sea voyagings are over. But you will find all these words in any old story of the sea. Charles Dibdin was himself a sailor, so that when he wrote poems about ships and sailors, and he wrote many, he knew what he was talking about. How clearly too he makes us *see* this jolly, handsome, faithful, kind-hearted young sailor—loved and mourned by everybody, shipmates and sweetheart.

[139] THE BURIAL OF SIR JOHN MOORE AT CORUNNA, 1809

In war there may be no time even to honour the dead—not even a great soldier such as Moore was. Those who had fought under him could but dig a hole by night with their bayonets, wrap him in his war-cloak, bid him farewell, and sail away 'on the billow' to sea. His enemies might 'upbraid' or blame him, even when his body was dust and 'ashes.' *They* would always love him and would treasure his memory.

[140] SOLDIER, REST! THY WARFARE O'ER

Lines 6 to 8 mean that the hands of the unseen ones—the gentle spirits—watching over the soldier who is now at peace, will strew his bed with their flowers, while their unheard voices sing him to rest softly as dew falling upon leaf or grass. 'Rude' (verse 2) means loud and rough. 'Pibroch' is the battle-call of the bag-pipes. 'Fallow' is land that has been ploughed, but which will not be sown with seed for a year. The bittern is a bird that loves marshy places and 'sedgy shallows' by streams of water. His cry sounds like a faint hollow bellowing or drumming, and he is a secret bird. But now his strange voice is very seldom heard in England, because he has been hunted out of it by men with guns and by egg-robbers.

[141] THE QUESTION

This poem tells of a day-dream. Its last three words, which are spoken to the loved one referred to in the last line of the first stanza, give it its name. You will notice how *like* a dream it all is. Only in dreams will winter with its leafless trees and cold skies 'suddenly' be changed to spring. Shelley, too, in telling his dream, says that though many of the lovely flowers in it resembled those of the real world, they were all of them 'fairer' and lovelier than any that *wakened* eyes ever behold. They were 'visionary' flowers, that is *dream*-flowers, and with the light of dreams shining on them—on the eglantine and 'moonlight-coloured' may, and on the flower-cups, filled with their bright dew or 'wine' before the heat of the sun drinks it up.

He calls the daisies 'pearled' or bedewed 'Arcturi,' because Arcturus is one of the northern stars which can be seen shining every night of the year over England—unless, of course, they are hidden by cloud or mist. Unlike other stars, Sirius, Vega, or the stars of Orion, Arcturus never 'sets.' So, too, wherever in early summer onwards, and sometimes even in the depth of winter, you find short grass, you are almost sure to see a daisy in blossom there; and a cluster of daisies is like a cluster of stars, or 'constellated' (verse 2). That is why a daisy is like Arcturus—it may be seen shining all but the whole year through. Shelley mentions this again in another poem called 'The Invitation'—'the daisy star that never sets, The windflowers and violets.' And like that word 'windflowers' (three syllables) the third stanza in 'The Question' must be read very slowly to get the beautiful flow of the lines.

I know of no poet who hasn't *seen* things very clearly—Keats, for example, tells of his 'bush of May-flowers with the bees about them,' his 'ardent marigolds,' his sweet peas 'on tip-toe for a flight,' his minnows 'staying their wavy bodies 'gainst the stream.' He says of hair in a faint wind, 'Thy hair soft-lifted by the winnowing wind,' and of small gnats dancing in the air of evening, 'borne aloft, Or sinking as the light wind lives or dies.'

But you will notice that these flowers and minnows and midges have not only been seen very clearly, but also that they have been seen with a lively and loving regard. Whatever you admire you look at with all yourself in your eyes; and your love for it adds to its beauty. It was said of Shakespeare, the greatest of this world's poets, that he 'knew everything because he loved everything'; and this, each one of them in his own degree, is true of all true poets.

When then we read what they have written, we see again what they have seen so clearly; but we see it through their eyes and share their intense interest in it. They have made their words say not only what they thought, but what they felt—what intent and loving eyes have seen, what keen ears have heard, keen nose has smelt, and sensitive fingers have touched. This is one of the many strange and half-secret things that the reading of poetry does for us; and we can delight in it, and in the sounds of the words that tell of it, even when we do not wholly understand everything they may *mean*.

For the *sounds* of the words of poetry resemble the sounds of music. They are a pleasure and delight merely to listen to, as they rise and fall and flow and pause and echo—like the singing of birds at daybreak or a little before the fall of night when the daffodils 'take the winds of March with beauty.' It is a great pleasure also to *say* the words aloud—as well and clearly and carefully as one possibly can: 'green cowbind and the moonlight coloured may,' or 'flowers azure, black, and streaked with gold.' Try it.

I have always found, even after reading a poem twenty times, that the next time I read it there was not only a new meaning to be found in it, but also a new music—something I had not noticed before. For as we ourselves change and become a little different every year—and grow older every day—so poems change with us. In reading a poem we turn its words into something of our own. This indeed is the *only* way we can get anything out of any book. And the more of ourselves, of our senses, and feelings and dreams and thoughts and what we love and what we hope for, and what we believe in, we put into the words of a poem, by so much the better will that poem be.

When I was seven I loved rhymes and jingles. When I was fourteen I thought I hated poetry, partly perhaps because I had been made to learn it for a punishment. When I was about fifteen I suddenly *realised* that when the poet Homer said that his great hero, Achilles, in his rage went out 'black as night' he *meant* black as *night*. It was like a flash of summer lightning over a lovely country of hills and forests. From that day on, I think, I delighted in poetry more and more.

[143] A NOSEGAY

These few lines, which should be read (to run easily) with a little pause on Cullam*bine* for the rhyme's sake, are taken from a long poem called *The Shepherd's Calendar*, which was written about 1579, when Shakespeare was a boy of fourteen. I have kept the old spelling, as it seems to make the flowers smell all the sweeter, and it will also show how different Edmund Spenser's way was from our own. You could *choose* your spelling in those days; the name Shakespeare, for example, has been found spelt in over thirty different ways. Here the 'cullambine' is the columbine—the flower like four tiny doves drinking. 'Gelliflowres' are Gillyflowers (July-flowers) or spice-smelling stocks; 'Coronations' (*five* syllables here) are carnations; 'Sops in wine' are pinks (given by one 'paramour' or sweetheart to another); the pretty 'Pawnce' is the pansy, the 'Chevisaunce' may be the wallflower, unless the word was made up merely for the sake of the rhyme! The 'flowre Delice' or fleur-de-lis or flower-de-luce is the iris.

For flowers that 'sweeten the air with their breath' there is nothing like the white double violet and the musk rose—also pinks, wallflowers and honeysuckles; and for herbs, some of which—like mint, whose scent refreshes not only the nose but the mind—are sweet when crushed in the hand, we have—

> Rosemary green,
> And lavender blue,
> Thyme and sweet marjoram,
> Hyssop and rue.

[143] SPRING

The second and third lines mean, Now break or 'burgeon' into little green leaf-buds every tangle of quick-set hedge about the fields, where the white-thorns or May-trees are already in bloom, quick-set meaning, planted with *live* slips of thorn trees.

These few stanzas are part of a long poem called *In Memoriam*, which was written by Alfred Tennyson in memory of a friend who had died. They are brimful of the spring. Who has not seen, when winter is over and the woodlands are ringing with the songs of birds, that 'lovelier hue'—a faint purple—far across the fields above the woodlands. Then the lark climbs so high into the blue that though you can hear his faint, wild, shrill notes, like water-drops falling into a fountain, you cannot see him—it is 'a sightless song.' So full of life, too, is the spring, with its blossoming trees and hedges, its birds, and lambs and flowers—that it brings its comfort even to a grieving heart—'and my regret Becomes an April violet.'

232

[144] THE ROOKS

The more closely you read this the more clearly you will see—
see in your *mind*, not only the marvellous picture its words give
with their music, but how *true* the poem is. In its description, I
mean, of a 'legion' or multitude of rooks wheeling up into the
Italian skies at dawn, and filling the heavens with their harsh
voices in a 'pæan' or shout of joy, and then all streaming away
together through the mountain mists until out of sight. The
word 'grain' in line 11 here means the colour of the feathery or
plume-like clouds in the radiance of daybreak.

[145] THE BROOK

Sit quietly some early summer morning by a little brook or
stream and look about you, and think of where it has come from
and where it is going to, its 'herns,' or herons, the thorps or little
villages on its banks, its fields green with wheat or barley, shining
and whispering in the sun, or left fallow or wild for a time, its
fish and its birds, and the lulling music of its stony water—and
then you will see how wonderfully the words of this poem tell
of all this. It is almost as if its 'chattering' chiming water were
talking of its own sweet will.

[148] ELVES' SONG

Just nonsense—and it wants its music, but you can *see* the
mischievous faces of the elves peeping out through the words
like sunbeams in a poplar tree.

[149] A DROP OF DEW

Orient means eastern, and this drop of dew is shining in the
light of daybreak when the sun is in the east. It rests on its rose-
petal—scarcely touching it—as round and clear as a lucent ball of
crystal, enclosing in itself, as it were, the colours of the skies
above it. Any fine early May or June morning you can see dew-
drops lovely as this on grass and thorn and leaf and flower—
particularly on lupins and leeks. And could there be a lovelier
way of saying this than Andrew Marvell's?

[150] THE FRUIT PLUCKER

This has all the light and strangeness of the world of dreams—
that solitary moonlit wilderness with its strange fruits and the
'beauteous Boy,' wandering there among its fruits and flowers,
his only dress a 'cincture' or girdle or 'twine' of green leaves.

It is the darkest hour of the night—that before the break of dawn.
Then strange dreams and fears haunt the mind as we lie sick
and feverish and unable to sleep. Even the room and the things
we know and love best seem strange and 'gaunt' and terrifying—
as 'the sick child' in this poem tells his anxious mother. She
comforts him and is herself comforted to hear the market-carts
stirring in the streets beneath her window. Soon the first gleam
of daybreak will show in the sky, and the blue of morning
shine.

[152] THE NIGHTINGALE

When many nightingales are in a grove or wood, they seem to
be singing one against another—just as soldiers in a 'skirmish'
(line 11) call out as they fight. The nightingales' notes come
welling out of their bills in little trills and eddies—'capricious
passagings.' In this way they 'provoke' or challenge one another
to sing.

So bold is this bird when he sings to his hidden mate in her
nest that, to listen, you can stand close under the very twig on
which he is perched without alarming him. Nor does he sing
only in the dark, though of course when all other birds are
silent, except perhaps the willow-wren or the nightjar or the
woodlark or the owl, you hear his sweet wild voice more clearly
then. I remember once watching a nightingale singing in the
middle of the morning on a hedge in a churchyard, while the
other small birds that were perched quietly around him seemed
actually to be listening as closely to the notes babbling on and on
as I was myself. And once—it was a very hot and still afternoon—
as with a friend I passed by a flowering bush of gorse I heard
the tiniest of beautiful voices, so tiny that it seemed to come from
very far away. It was a nightingale *practising* his song.

[153] A COMPARISON

A *very* little stress on its three last words will give the run or lilt
of the first line. The 'briar' of course is the *sweet* briar, which
smells even sweeter after rain. 'Nard' or spikenard has a delicious
scent too—when it is heated. And 'the bag of the bee' is the
little pouch on its thigh in which it carries the pollen from the
flowers to make 'bee-bread.'

As we grow old, sleep does not always come so quickly as it did when we were young—that sleep which not only, as this poem says, 'binds' up the mind (as if with a 'chain') from thinking, but is also, as many other poets have said, rest and peace from the cares and troubles of the day. It is then that memories return to us, happy or sad, of the days that are gone. I remember some years ago talking to a very old watchman one winter's night as he sat in his little cabin in front of a blazing fire on a road that was being mended with new flints. He told me that he only slept a few hours during the day when his long night watch was over, and he spoke of 'the blissful plains of Paradise'—words which, so far as I know, were his own way of saying what he meant by them.

The next few poems also tell of the sadness of parting from those we love, and being absent from them, or far from home, and the gladness of the coming back again.

[154] ABSENCE

'Eerie' here means forlorn—so forlorn that it is as if the heavy hours themselves were 'wae' or sad now that she is gone. 'Wasna sae' is the Scots way of saying the English, *was not so*.

[154] ROBIN ADAIR

A song of grief for one who is gone, but will never be forgotten. 'The assembly' is the place where the people met together to dance at the 'ball.'

[157] VAILIMA

Owing to ill health, Stevenson, who was the author of many enthralling tales of adventure—*Treasure Island* and *Kidnapped* among them—spent the last years of his life at 'Vailima' in Samoa, an island in the South Seas. In this poem he is thinking of his old home, and seeing it in memory so clearly—its moors and their 'howes' or valleys, now in shower now in sunshine, with their flat or 'recumbent' tombstones, beneath which rest the bones of its ancient races—he sees it all so clearly and with such longing that it is as if his own ghost were wandering there again. 'Whaups' (line 3) are curlews or peewits, lovely in flight and with a wild, sweet, mournful call or cry.

[159] OPHELIA'S SONG

'Larded' means covered over; and when in days long gone by

you saw a man, staff in hand and a 'cockle' or *scallop*-shell (one of the most beautiful of all shells) sewn upon his hat, you knew he was a pilgrim, and had journeyed either to Palestine or to one of the sacred shrines or holy places of the world. Any such journey then meant long travel and hardship.

[159] THE SHOWER

The thorny acacia tree—under which the young organ-grinder stands with his carved and painted organ, as if under a huge umbrella—grows very tall and gracefully and has dark-green narrow leaves dangling in pairs (like the ash) which bud late in the spring and fall soon after summer. Its long clusters of sweet white flowers are tasselled like the laburnum's; and at the cool of evening each leaf folds itself gently towards the one nearest it, like the clover, and goes to sleep.

[161] THE STORM

Listen next time you watch the clouds of a thunderstorm passing away among the distant hills, and you will discover how strangely *true* lines 7 and 8 are.

[161] THE POPLAR FIELD

A row of Lombardy poplars stands up straight and tall like the marble columns or pillars of a 'colonnade.' They shine in the spring like green torches of the sun, and their heart-shaped leaves twirl and whisper at the least stir of the wind. *These* poplars— that once grew on the banks of the river Ouse—after being loved and delighted in for twelve years have been 'felled' or cut down. And the writer of the verses grieves to see them gone. Listen carefully to the sound of the words as they flow and falter on from line to line.

[162] ONE LIME

The fresh honey-sweet fragrance of the 'lime' or linden tree has a curious way of lying in the still, warm air of summer like invisible pools of water; you can almost taste it—like the bees.

[162] THE WHIRL-BLAST

A 'bower' is a little house of leafy branches; 'myriads' (line 18) means thousands upon thousands (dancing in the hail); and Robin Goodfellow is yet another name for the impish fairy, Puck, or Hobgoblin, who is so busy by moonlight on page 113.

[163] TO AUTUMN

There are many poems that tell of the flowers and birds and life

236

and loveliness of Spring and Summer, and of the magical frost and snows and winds of Winter. This one is in praise of Autumn, the 'season of mists' at dawn and at the close of evening, and the long quiet twilight of the shortening days. Yet they are days so brimful of light and warmth that they seem, as the poem says, to be 'bosom-friends' of the sun. This too is the season when the grapes are 'maturing' or ripening, and the apples, the gourds and the hazel-nuts too. The later flowers of the year, though winter draws near, are also blossoming, and so many of them as they unfold shine out in the autumn sunbeams that it seems as if the bees will be able to go on and on for weeks together, gathering the nectar for the brimming honey that will be their food when the cold and 'slow dark hours begin.'

In the second verse it is as though we saw the very ghost of autumn herself as she sits resting awhile from her harvest work on the floor of the granary in which the corn is laid up for the winter; or sleeping in the wheat fields, her sickle in her hand; or watching the 'last oozings' of the juice from the apples in the cider-press, as they drop, drop, drop, drop in the still sunshine.

As for the third and last verse, it is the quietest and fullest description of an autumn evening in the country that I know. In these few lines we are given nearly everything—the rosy clouds, 'blooming' in straight lines or 'bars' as they often do, against the gold or pale green of the western sky, the evening midges among the 'sallows' or osiers by the waterside, the lambs, the swallows—that we have ever seen or heard when 'looking on the happy autumn fields, And thinking of the days that are no more.'

[164] THE EQUINOX

Towards the end of March, and again towards the end of September, it is twelve hours between the rising of the sun in the east and his setting in the west; and another twelve hours will pass by before he rises again. So at this season the nights and the days are equal, and they are called days of the 'equinox.' It is then, after the quiet of summer, that the storm-winds begin to blow across the enormous stretches of the Atlantic; and there is the roar and surge of wind and water in the very sound of this poem.

Like nearly all poems it is best read aloud. Then you can not only *hear* the words better than you can when you are reading

237

them to yourself, but you also have the pleasure of *making* them with your tongue and lips and throat, just as the singer has the pleasure of singing as well as of hearing himself sing. Anyhow, the louder this poem is read the better. When next a south-west gale comes, begin: 'When-descends-on-the-*Atlantic*' and see who can shout the loudest. And after that you might look up 'Bermuda's reefs,' and the islands of the Azores and the Hebrides, in an atlas. *That* won't spoil the poem; for nearly every name in the maps of that atlas has a story to it, and one very often packed with romance and courage and adventure. Find out too, what 'skerries' are, and why the sea is called the 'main.'

[167] WINTER

The 'earth's universal face' (line 10) means the wide, wild stretch of wooded country now, as far as the eye can reach, lying cold and deep in snow. 'Hoar' (line 8) means white as hoar-frost, and the ox (line 12) is called the labourer because in the days when this poem was written oxen were used to plough with, as they still are in other countries. Here he 'demands' or lows for his food, or wages. Lines 14 to 20 tell how most of the wild birds in winter flock to the farmyard to pick up what grain they can from the barns and stacks. But the robin, that has for centuries been kept 'sacred' even by those who have little care for other birds, and that knows all about the weather—the cold or stormy or 'embroiling sky'—posts off to the farmhouse kitchen, its merry firelight shining at the window, and even goes hopping in over the flagstones to pick up crumbs. With his round dark bright eye he looks at the children sideways or 'askance.' All this might perhaps have been said a little more simply in the poem, but many of the poets in the eighteenth century had a habit of saying things in James Thomson's way, and an excellent way for its own *purpose* it usually was.

[168] BLOW, BLOW

The meaning of this song is rather doleful, and yet the song itself is in a very merry key. When the bleak winter wind blows we cannot *see* what is biting our cheeks and noses and fingers—only pigs can see the wind!—and we don't feel it or mind it so much as when friends are unkind and their love is only feigning or a sham. Besides, this song, like 'Under the Greenwood Tree' (page 147), comes from the play called *As You Like It*, and is sung

238

in the forest of Arden where, even though the wintry wind blows cold and every pool is frozen hard, 'Green grows the holly, O!' and a good song soon warms up the blood.

[168] A THANKSGIVING TO GOD FOR HIS HOUSE

Robert Herrick, after living in London and knowing many of the poets who knew Shakespeare, went down into Devonshire. He was a clergyman and had his church there, and his little parsonage near it, and this poem is about the parsonage, his 'cell' as he calls it. He thanks God for everything in it, though he lives a very simple life, 'void of state,' for that is his fate or fortune in this world. 'Spars' (line 5) means the beams or rafters over his head, which were left bare before plaster ceilings came into use. Later on in the poem (line 28), 'pulse' means peas or beans, 'worts' are roots (potatoes, turnips, carrots), and 'purslane' is a kind of salad which he added to his little heap or 'mess' of water cress. 'Soils' means to enrich. Instead of wine his cows give him milk and cream—'conduits' meaning hollow stone troughs for water to run along. 'A thankful heart . . . fired with incense' means a heart fragrant with peace and joy—incense being made of spices and gums which smell sweet when they smoulder. I am not quite sure what 'unfled' (line 22) means; perhaps it means unspoiled or with crusts unbroken; or unnibbled—by the mice.

[170] THE YEAR'S ROUND

If you look at the petals of the yellow or 'saffron' crocus blossoming in the cold winds of February or March, you will see not only their fine lines or veinings, but their shininess or sheen. 'Crude' (line 3) here means rough and the next line means that the bark, as spring advances, shows or reveals its green leaf-buds as bright and tiny as gems or emeralds. When the frost of winter comes at nightfall you can actually *watch* its tiny 'silver bars' creeping across the surface of a puddle, changing or transmuting its water into ice.

[171] THE WIFE OF USHER'S WELL

There are more than three hundred Scottish ballads, most of them centuries old. In other books you will find many almost as simple and lovely as this one. I say simple, though until one is used to their Scots words and spelling, they are a little hard to follow.

This ballad tells how a mother, no longer young, for she is called 'the carline wife,' which means old woman, had three sons, and you can't have better riches than that, for they were fine and sturdy young men, 'stout and stalwart.' They went to sea and in but a few weeks their ship was wrecked, and they were drowned. While that wild tempest is still blowing, their old mother hears this bitter news, and in her grief she cannot believe it. She prays to God in her heart only that she may see her three sons again, and see them soon: 'May this wind (she says) continue to blow, making trouble in the sea—"fashes in the flood"—until my three sons come back to me.' But it is as travellers from the far country of Paradise, and not 'in earthly flesh and blood,' that at last at Martinmas, the feast of St. Martin, November 11th, they visit her; and on their heads are garlands of the little green leaves of the heavenly 'birk' or birch-tree that never grew in its silver by any earthly 'syke' or 'sheugh'— by any green ditch or watercourse, that is—but at the very gates of Paradise itself. She welcomes them, and bids her maidens blow up the fire while she herself makes up a bed for them. And she sits down to watch all night beside them. But dawn breaks— the dawn that calls all spirits home to their own place. They hear cock-crow from out of the grey mists beyond the window, summoning them away; and though it grieves them bitterly to leave their old mother, knowing how wild her sorrow will be when she awakes to find them gone, they must obey. And in silence as they came, so in silence they go.

I am uncertain of the meaning of the eleventh verse, but it *may* be 'The channerin' worm doth chide' means that *conscience*, which is as wise as the serpent, is reproaching them for delaying to go when they know they ought to go; while if they refuse to obey its voice, then sore will be the punishment they will 'abide' or endure—even so near this side of the gates of Paradise. Or it may mean the worm that in the grave 'destroys this mortal *body*.'

[172] THE DREAM

This poem is a rather clumsy old English version of 'The Wife of Usher's Well.' It is almost as different from the last as a bed-post is from a birch-tree. But for this very reason, and because they tell the same kind of story, it is interesting to compare them.

[174] AS JOSEPH WAS AWAKENING

'A-wauking' (line 1) means either keeping watch or awakening—from sleep and dreams or *visions* of the night. 'Housen' (line 6) is an old form of the English plural, like oxen; and 'usen,' of the verb, i.e. *that is used for all babies.*

[175] I SING OF A MAIDEN

Taken out of its ancient English spelling, the meaning of the first verse of this lovely old carol is: 'I sing of a maiden, who is solitary in her beauty and blessedness; she chose for her son the King of Kings.' For the sake of the rhyme, the April in each stanza should be said with a very slight accent on the second syllable as well as on the first; as we say *re-fill*. Makeless is three syllables; Godes (God's), two.

[178] THE PILGRIM

John Bunyan was a brazier by trade, and when a boy of seventeen fought in the battle of Naseby. He spent twelve years in prison for preaching what he believed to be the true Gospel. He was the author of a great many books, and while he was in prison a second time wrote what is perhaps the best-loved book in English, *The Pilgrim's Progress*.

This is his poem about a pilgrim. The very tramp of the words puts courage into one's heart; they have the ring and thunder of drums and trumpets. 'Shall make him once relent His first-avowed intent' means, shall make him regret even for a moment the solemn promise he made at the beginning to be a pilgrim. Be sure in reading, whether aloud or to yourself, to make 'lion' and 'giant' just two syllables.

[179] TO A WATERFOWL

I am not sure what *kind* of waterfowl is meant in this poem. But the bird I have always seen when reading it is the heron. It loves to wade or stand for hours fishing on the 'plashy' brink or edge of the waters of a lake or on the 'marge' or grassy shore of a river, and it flies with a low, slow sweep of its wide wings. In the poem it is evening, and the sky is rosy with sunset, with 'the last steps of day.' On high, far beyond the reach of the fowler, the solitary bird floats on through the cold, thin, rare, empty, 'desert' air of twilight until in the deep-blue sky, 'the abyss of heaven,' it vanishes and is gone.

[180] EPITAPH ON A JACOBITE

An inscription written on the stone above a grave in memory of the dead is called an epitaph, and 'Jacobite' was the name given to the loyal and faithful followers of King James II (the Latin for James being Jacobus), who after reigning for a few years gave up his throne and went into exile from England, never to return. *This* Jacobite, as his epitaph declares, gave up everything, even his home itself, in loyalty to his king, to live out the rest of his short, unhappy life in a strange land. And lovely though Italian Lavernia and the river Arno were, beside which he dwelt, he dreamed every night of that home in England, and ever mourned to see again what was to him her lovelier Tees. Yet of those who should chance to read his epitaph he asked only this: *Forget all feuds: Quiet all quarrels.* So may it be with us—ourselves and all nations!

[181] KING CHARLES

James II was in much a bad and cruel king; and Charles I, his father, was a brave, but not always wise, and an unhappy one. But there were many who loved him loyally and devotedly. One of these (in the poem), a country-man perhaps, seeing his beautiful 'black' bronze statue—that stands to this day where once stood one of the carved stone crosses set up by Edward I in remembrance of his beloved queen, Eleanor—asks, 'Who is that?' And in his love and loyalty is grieved beyond all words at being told who it is. Only four lines—and our own hearts, whether we share that love or not, share all his grief. The King was beheaded one wintry morning in the courtyard of White-hall, on January 30, 1649.

[181] THE SPRING IS PAST

These verses were written in the Tower of London by Chidiock Tichborne the night before he was beheaded for plotting against Queen Elizabeth; he was then a young man still in his twenties.

[183] A HIGH TIDE ON THE COAST OF LINCOLNSHIRE

The story in this clear, lovely and tragic poem is told in a rather roundabout way, though as soon as it is understood, it is shown to be an excellent way.

When—on that distant Saturday evening which the poem tells of—high tide was at its fullest on the low, flat coast of Lincolnshire, an immense rushing wave or 'eygre' (verse 14) with foaming crest came towering in from the sea towards the land. To warn the people, far inland, of their dreadful danger, the bell-ringers of Boston rang out a wild peal of alarm. The mayor himself, old man though he was, climbed up into the high steeple after them.

In the second verse it is a mother who is speaking. She remembers—as she sat spinning in her doorway that peaceful evening long ago—how her thread broke off, and she lifted her eyes and saw the blood-red sun—red as 'ore' or molten metal from the fire—sinking, and at the same moment both saw and heard in the distance not only the swanherds who kept the swans, and the shepherd boys with their sheep, but also her 'son's fair wife, Elizabeth' whom she dearly loved, wandering by the little River Lindis with its rich meads or meadows of 'melick' grass, and calling home the cows. Then suddenly she heard the alarm bells clang out from the towering church steeple a full five miles away. But many who heard them could find no reason for this wild ringing. It could not, they argued, be pirates as in the old days, or a shipwreck beyond the 'scorp' or sea-cliff, since it was dead calm. And suddenly, her son comes riding in 'with might and main'—as hard as his horse can gallop—wildly crying his dreadful warning, and shouting 'Elizabeth! Elizabeth!' Too late he sees her and her two 'bairns' or children playing happily together on the banks of the Lindis, for already the dread eygre or tidal wave is thundering on its way, sweeping everything before it over the flat meadows. And in a moment, 'all the world'—as far as the eye can reach—is under water 'in the sea.'

The rest of the poem, I think, from 'So farre, so fast' (verse 16) is quite plain—though it will need, as all poetry needs, eye, mind and heart to be intent on it.

The spelling is only a little different from usual; 'bin' means is; 'mote' means might; 'flow' (verse 20) means flood-tide; and 'pied' (verse 2) means black and white, as in the word magpie; the 'mews' were sea-gulls.

There is another poem of Jean Ingelow's almost as clear and wild, and tender as this, 'When Sparrows Build.' She herself was born at Boston on March 17th, 1820, and there is something in her poetry that faintly reminds me of Emily Brontë's (who was born in Yorkshire in 1818), though *her* genius as a poet was beyond that of any other woman's, even Christina Rossetti's.

[189] KEITH OF RAVELSTON

'One of the most perfectly beautiful ghost stories I know; poetry in every line and every word.' This is what Alice Meynell said of this poem, and she, a poet too, delighted in poetry with all her mind and all her heart. The 'maid' in the poem was watching over her mother's 'kine' or cows that Monday morning when first Andrew Keith, with his 'henchmen' or squires and servants, came riding down by the silver-blossoming thorn-tree in whose shade she sat. He was of a long 'line' or lineage—that is, of an old and noble family that could remember what had happened to its ancestors in the years long gone by, many of them tragic and sorrowful things. That is all we are told of them both while she was alive. And when she is dead, her quiet ghost haunts the solitary place at evening, where she was both happy and sorrowful, and the 'burnie' or little stream babbles by, telling much but saying nothing.

[193] FEAR NO MORE

This comes from a play called *Cymbeline*. It is a 'dirge' or song of mourning sung over the grave of the lovely and faithful Imogen, who when she disguised herself in boy's clothes to journey alone to meet her husband, called herself Fidele. Like Snow-White in the old tale she was not really dead, only in a deep swoon. The poem tells how, when life is over, none can harm us, even if they would; and our work is done. In this, old or young, rich or poor, we are all alike. The king (verse 2) must lay down his 'sceptre,' the scholar must shut up his books of 'learning'; the doctor has no more use for his 'physic'—we have gone home, all earthly sorrows over, all 'joy and moan,' and have taken our last wages, for after all our 'worldly tasks' are finished there comes the peace of the grave.

[194] COME UNTO THESE YELLOW SANDS

Here beside a sea so calm and 'whist' that there is not the falling of the least wave to break the silence, the fairies are featly, nimbly dancing.

[194] THE OLD SHIPS

I won't attempt to explain all that this beautiful poem tells of the old ships lying becalmed in the Adriatic. Or of that still older ship which carried Ulysses away, more than twenty centuries ago, when the walls of the city of Troy had fallen, and it had been captured by the Greeks hidden in their great wooden horse. But it is well worth while to find out about it.

As John Ruskin said, never let a word escape you that looks 'suspicious,' that you are not quite *sure* you understand. It is hard work sometimes to get at the meaning of a word, but it is often better to do it for yourself than to ask someone who knows it already, for it is work that soon becomes interesting and at last a real pleasure. In any case, find it out, somehow, if you possibly can.

[195] DRAKE'S DRUM

The great Admiral Drake was 'a Devon man,' and the words of this poem—full of the sea and light and music—are spelt as a man of Devon would say them.

[197] THE FAIRY THORN

Apart from a few unusual words, there is nothing very hard to follow in this story of the Fairy Thorn (an old Irish ballad) if it is read slowly and carefully. Listen to it, as you say it or read it, and *see* all it tells of in your mind. 'Rock' in the second verse means the distaff of Anna's spinning-wheel. The red-berried rowan-tree (verse 4) is what is generally called in England a mountain ash; and when it is hung with its tassels of bright berries it is a beautiful thing to see, particularly in morning sunshine. 'Braes' (verse 7) are the smooth green slopes and valleys of a hillside, and 'shaws' (verse 8) are little clustered woods or thickets.

If, between finger and thumb, you very gently draw out a curling lock of hair, it will as gently spring back when you release it; and that, I think, is what 'curls elastic' (verse 13) means.

There is a very beautiful and much longer poem, resembling this one, called 'Goblin Market,' by Christina Rossetti.

[200] LA BELLE DAME SANS MERCI

'Fragrant zone' means a girdle of sweet-smelling wild flowers. 'Manna dew' means dew divinely clear and refreshing. 'Elfin' means fairy; and 'La Belle Dame sans Merci' is 'the lovely but pitiless Lady.'

Index of Authors

Index of First Lines

ABOUT THE AUTHOR

WALTER DE LA MARE, poet, novelist, short-story writer, critic, dramatist, and anthologist, was born in Kent in 1873. For many years he earned his living as a statistician in the office of the Anglo-American Oil Company. In 1908 the British government awarded him a small pension and thus set him free to devote all his energies to writing. Few writers of any period have equalled his record for writing inspired verse over a very long period. An artist of complete integrity, he never considered the demands of the market. Mr. de la Mare died at his home in Twickenham, England, on June 22, 1956.

A NOTE ON THE TYPE

The text of this book has been set on the Monotype
in a type face named *Aldine Bembo*. The roman is
a copy of a letter cut for the celebrated Venetian
printer Aldus Manutius by Francesco Griffo, and
first used in Cardinal Bembo's De Aetna of 1495—
hence the name of the revival. Griffo's type is now
generally recognized, thanks to the researches of
Mr. Stanley Morison, to be the first of the old face
group of types. The companion italic is an adapta-
tion of a chancery script type designed by the
Roman calligrapher and printer Lodovico degli
Arrighi, called Vincentino, and used by him
during the 1520's.

Composed in England. Printed by Rae Lithog-
raphers, Cedar Grove, New Jersey. Bound by
Charles H. Bohn, New York.